Dog TRICKS

Step by Step

Mary Ann Rombold Zeigenfuse
and Jan Walker

Howell Book House
New York

Howell Book House
A Simon & Schuster Macmillan Company
1633 Broadway
New York, NY 10019

MACMILLAN is a registered trademark of Macmillan, Inc.

Zeigenfuse, Mary Ann Rombold.
 Dog Tricks: Step by Step/Mary Ann Rombold Zeigenfuse & Jan Walker.
 ISBN: 0–87605–593–5
 1. Dog—Training. I. Walker, Jan (Janet Sue) II. Title.
SF431.Z45 1997
636.7'0888—dc21 97–7686
CIP
Manufactured in the United States of America

0 1 2/0 10 9 8 7 6 5 4

Design by Amy Peppler Adams—designLab, Seattle

*In Memory of my Dad,
William M. Rombold
and my dog, Bosé.
Dad was the first trickster in my life.
Bosé was "the wind beneath my wings."*

Contents

Acknowledgments

There was a time when I thought I might have been adopted. Not that that would have been bad, but it seemed to me that I was the only one in my family who was infatuated with dogs. I had only one dream as a child and that was to own a dog. This was not shared by any other member of my family. I thought I was a misfit. This thought stayed with me until only recently. On a visit to my home town, I went to see my Uncle Fred and Aunt Ann. Uncle Fred was my father's older brother and one of my favorite people growing up. One of the reasons was that he always had a dog; so to visit Uncle Fred meant also play with a dog. During the visit, Uncle Fred was catching me up on the family news; this information was presented with love and interest, but no pictures. Then he started to tell me about a dog that lived in the neighborhood where he and my aunt summered in Florida. He told me how he walked the dog every day and what a great friend this dog had become. You guessed it: This is when the pictures came out. He had pictures of the dog walking with him and of the dog alone. My heart just squeezed. It was like coming home. In my home I could show you snap shots of every dog I know, but don't ask to see pictures of my friends and relatives. Those would take a lot more time to put my hands on. So, Uncle Fred, thank you for letting me be part of your family.

The other important people in my life who have made me feel like family are Jack and Wendy Volhard. They understand dogs, people, and how to communicate with both. They are true teachers. They want to give everyone everything they know and have to offer. They have taught me so much and have taken me under their wing. At the same time, they have pushed me to be what I can and to do it on my own. Without them as my mentors, I wouldn't be writing to you and I couldn't have been here. Thank you Jack and Wendy for "adopting" me.

Then there are the dogs. So many dogs have taught me so much, sometimes baffling me, sometimes humoring me, but always allowing me into their lives and their hearts. I meet many dogs every day, and each is so honest in approach and so willing to play along with whatever I dish out. I thank them all and look forward to meeting tomorrow's dogs.

Some of the dogs in my life are pictured in this book. They are:

> Nipper-T, a Yorkshire Terrier, owned by myself and my husband, Robert Zeigenfuse.
>
> Clay, a yellow Labrador, owned by Casey Eckert.
>
> Lil Bit, an Australian Shepherd, owned by Ann Keller.
>
> Sparky, an All-American, owned by Diane and Allen Haughey.
>
> Sadie, a chocolate Labrador, owned by Mary Margaret Sterling.
>
> Orco, a Border Collie, owned by Ann Keller.
>
> Zoo, an All-American, owned by Diane and Allen Haughey.
>
> Fresco, a black Labrador, owned by Barb Koetsier.
>
> Muppy, an All-American, owned by Pat Graham.
>
> Chica, owned by Monica Udvardy and Thomas Hakånsson.
>
> Shana, a Border Collie, owned by Sharon Shepard.
>
> Zack, a Viszla, owned by Lisa Hamblen.

I would also like to thank my sister, Tamara Yohannes, who allowed me to bounce everything off her for this book. This was a true gift to me, since as I said before, I am the only real dog person in my family. Thanks, Tamara.

Introduction

Capitalize on your dog's talents.

First and foremost, we have our dogs as companions. Our dogs bring us joy, and as any proud parent would be with a child, showing off our dogs to the world is far more fun then anyone can imagine. We can show them off for their good looks, for their charm and cuteness, and for their talents and skills.

This book will show you how to capitalize on your dog's natural talents, enhance your dog's instinctive behaviors, and possibly even make

1

Some dogs get shown for their looks.

your dog famous by performing new and attention-getting tricks. The fame may only reach as far as your living room, or it may take you all the way to stardom, but either way, it will take your dog deep into your heart.

Most dogs will be able to learn *all* of the tricks in this book. By using the Canine Personality Test that follows, you will see which tricks are best suited for *your* individual dog, and which ones will be easiest for your dog to learn. This is your own recipe for a built-in success formula.

Would you like your dog to Bob for Apples, or Sneeze on Command? What about a dog that can Wake Up the Kids or go Trick or Treating with you? A personal favorite is any dog that can Find the Remote Control or play Hide and Seek.

What ever it is that you want your dog to learn, you can teach it. With the help from this book, you can learn the important steps to teaching the dog just about anything. Having fun while you and your dog practice is what this book is all about. Let your imagination be your limitation.

Make your dog a star.

Show off your dog's natural talents.

Chapter ONE

Let's Start Tonight

You can start right away, tonight, teaching your dog the first trick. You will need a start to the trick, which is the *command*, and an end to the trick, called the *release*. You can praise all through the performance, so don't use your praise words as the end to a trick. The release word can be "OK," which will signal that work is finished and your dog will now get a reward. The reward can be anything the dog likes: petting from you, getting a cookie (dog treat), or playing with a favorite toy. Whatever the reward is, your dog really needs to know that work is finished when you say "OK."

So remember, each trick has:

1. A **Command,** which signals your dog what to do.

2. **Praise** during the performance.

3. A **Release Word,** which ends the trick.

4. A **Reward** or something your dog likes.

"The Release," which ends the trick.

5

Wag Your Tail

An easy first trick that all dogs can do, even those with just a stub of a tail, is to wag their tails on command. Your dog's tail probably already wags in response to pleasant and excited words from you.

You want to take your dog's natural "talent" of being happy when accompanying you and make it into a trick to be performed on command. By starting with this trick, you can also start putting into practice the use of a command and a release word as well as praising your dog while working. *You want to capitalize on your relationship with your dog, for you are now a team.*

Praising your dog's performance will keep the tail wagging.

First decide on the *command* you want to use. It can be something simple like: "Bingo, wag your Tail," or a more philosophical question: "Bingo, are you a happy dog?" Once you have made up your mind, stick to it, for consistency's sake. You want your dog to learn your command. Say the command with a lot of enthusiasm in your voice, initially a happy, almost squeaky voice. Your dog will get excited and respond to your attention with tail wagging. *Praising your dog's performance will keep the tail wagging.* You can then release your dog by saying "OK" and giving a treat or a petting session. Try it again.

1 **Command** in a high and happy voice: "Are you a happy dog?"

2 **Praise** to get the tail really moving.

3 **Release** by saying: "OK."

4 **Reward** with a cookie or petting session.

Most likely your dog will get excited and want to do it over and over again. Remember you are trying to label your dog's chosen behavior, so make your command clear and different sounding from anything else you might say.

This is a **Prey Drive** trick because of the motivational, high-pitched tone of voice. Prey Drive is those behaviors based on the instinct to hunt, kill and feed. **Pack Drive** is also necessary because of the bond between you and your dog. You and your dog enjoying the togetherness of a learning situation is all part of being in and putting your dog in Pack Drive, which is based on social interaction with both humans and other animals. *(See the Drives Chapter for more information.)*

Each dog is born with a predetermined personality.

The age a puppy is when leaving the litter makes a big difference on the rest of the dog's life.

Your Dog's Personality

If you have more than one dog or have known more than one dog, you already appreciate that each dog is very different in personality. One dog likes to cuddle more than the other, one likes to play ball and the other doesn't, one will guard the house well and the other one will run when approached by a stranger. What makes each dog different?

Every dog, yours included, was born with a partially pre-determined personality. Your dog's experiences since birth have helped mold that personality. These experiences include how the mother raised the litter, and at what age each dog left the litter. These make a big difference. What experiences a pup has had during the critical periods of development have all influenced how your dog looks at the world and chooses to react to it. You can take a test and actually determine how a dog will react to the surrounding environment. This will tell you what your dog's Drives are, and will give you insight into what personality characteristics you will see.

Your dog's way of reacting to the world is instinctive. These instinctive behaviors can be broken into three categories or Drives: Prey Drive, Pack Drive, and Defense Drive. These Drives are referred to as natural talents

You can determine how your dog views the world.

because our dogs came pre-programmed with them. It is the concentration of each Drive that makes up each dog's personality.

You can test your dog and see how high the Drives are in each category. You can then determine how your dog looks at the world. It will help you to understand how your dog learns, and to know which exercises or tricks will be easier to accomplish and which may take a little longer to learn. This applies to formal Obedience as well as household training. It can help you recognize which tricks might be easier to teach based solely on your dog's Drives and Personality Profile.

Recoginze you dog's capabilities and answer each question honestly.

The Personality Test

Let's see how your dog's personality is arranged. Each category in this test has a set of questions. While taking the test for your dog you will need to answer each question honestly.

Answer according to what your dog would do if presented with the situation described in each question. If your dog would *almost always* react this way, score 10 points; for *sometimes,* score 5 points; or if you believe your dog would hardly ever do what the question says, score 0 points. *Points are neither bad nor good.* The total score will simply give you the proportions of the three Drives that your dog possesses. Notice that Defense Drive is divided into two categories, so they each get a set of questions.

Stealing food shows Prey Drive in action.

Canine Personality Test

Always: **10**   Sometimes: **5**   Hardly Ever: **0**

Personality / Behavior Questions.

Prey Drive
Does your dog:

1. Sniff the ground or air a lot? _____
2. Get excited by moving objects, such as bikes or squirrels? _____
3. Stalk cats, other dogs or things in the grass? _____
4. When excited, bark in a high-pitched voice? _____
5. Pounce on toys? _____
6. Shake and "kill" toys? _____
7. Steal food or garbage? _____
8. Like to carry things? _____
9. Wolf down food? _____
10. Like to dig and bury things? _____

Total for Prey Drive Section : _____

Pack Drive

Does your dog:

1. Get along with other dogs? _____
2. Get along with people? _____
3. Bark when left alone? _____
4. Solicit petting or like to snuggle with you? _____
5. Like to be groomed? _____
6. Seek eye contact with you? _____
7. Follow you around like a shadow? _____
8. Play a lot with other dogs? _____
9. Jump up to greet people? _____
10. Show reproductive behaviors, such as courting or mounting other dogs? _____

Total of Pack Drive Answers: _____

Jumping up to greet people is part of Pack Drive.

Defense/Fight Drive

Does your dog:

1. Stand its ground or investigate strange objects or sounds? _____

2. Like to play tug of war games to win? _____

3. Bark or growl in a deep tone? _____

4. Guard territory? _____

5. Guard food or toys? _____

6. Dislike being petted? _____

7. Guard the owner(s)? _____

8. Dislike being groomed or bathed? _____

9. Like to fight with other dogs? _____

10. Get picked on by other dogs
    (either now or when it was young)? _____

Total of Defense /Fight Responses: _____

Guarding is part of Defense/Fight Drive.

Defense/Flight Drive

Does your dog:

1. Run away from new situations? _____

2. Hide behind you when unable to cope? _____

3. Act fearful in unfamiliar situations? _____

4. Tremble or whine when unsure? _____

5. Crawl or turn upside down when reprimanded? _____

6. Reluctant to come close to you when called? _____

7. Have difficulty standing still when groomed? _____

8. Cringe when someone strange bends over him/her? _____

9. Urinate during greeting behavior? _____

10. Tend to bite when cornered? _____

Total of Defense/Flight Responses: _____

Dog exhibiting Defense/Fight with an intruder.

Versus a dog exhibiting Defense/Flight Drive.

As you can see by the questions themselves, each category tells a little about your dog's psychological makeup. Pack Drive shows your dog's willingness to be part of a pack or group that includes you. Prey Drive shows the instincts that helped dogs get food when they lived in the wild. Defense/Fight shows just that, the behaviors of defending with courage your dog's territory or space. Defense/Flight shows dogs' concern for their well being and that they would preferably leave during stressful situations if they could, just as you might wish the floor could open up and swallow you at times.

With few exceptions, dogs will have some of each Drive. They need all the Drives to survive in Nature. And even though we now provide their

We now provide our dogs' food, but they still need Prey Drive.

food, they still need Prey Drive to play and retrieve. We secure their safety, but they need Defense/Fight to be able to cope with pressures from hard work, like learning new things. And they need Pack Drive just to live in harmony with us. The need for Defense/Flight is not really evident in a domestic situation, but if a dog has a lot of Defense/Flight Drive, it is important to know it, because how we act toward a dog with a lot of Flight Drive will make or break that dog. A dog with high Flight Drive can be easily stressed and might live in constant turmoil if not provided with a consistent and stable environment.

The level of each Drive is what helps you to see into your dog's personality. Any number above 50 is considered high. Obviously the closer to 100, the higher the Drive. A dog can be high in all the Drives: Prey, Pack, and Defense (either Fight or Flight), or a dog can be high in only one, or in none. Lower than 30 is considered low in any Drive.

Being low in a Drive is not necessarily bad. Being high is not necessarily good. The numbers are simply teaching you about your dog. True, some Drives are more desirable for certain tasks. High Fight Drive is needed for a task requiring a dog with lots of confidence to work alone, like a guard dog or a guide dog. High Pack Drive would be desirable for a family pet or a therapy dog. High Prey Drive is needed for a good herding dog.

But as already mentioned, high is over 50 and too much of a good thing may not be so desirable either. A high Prey Drive dog may not be able to concentrate on the job at hand if the leaves in the trees are rustling. *Learn your dog* so you can be prepared for any situation that you are putting your dog into. *Know what to expect* from your dog so you won't be surprised or disappointed when your dog acts a certain way. *Learn to anticipate* how your dog will react by knowing your dog's Personality Profile.

Each trick in this book is marked as being easier for one Drive or another. Find those that are marked as being in a Drive that is *your dog's* highest, and start there for easy success, and then move on to others. *Any thing can be taught to any dog.* It is just a matter of understanding what Drive your dog is in, what Drive *you want* the dog to be in and knowing how to get there by switching your dog's Drives. Working hard and making it fun for you and your dog is the key.

It is important to be aware of your body language when dealing with dogs. When you lean forward and over a dog, it puts that dog into Defense Drive. Dogs high in Flight might run or flip over on their backs. If you lean backwards with your hands up, you will put a dog into Prey Drive. This is very

Guide dogs need lots of confidence, which they get from Defense/Fight Drive.

stimulating and can be helpful when trying to get a dog to jump over something. A neutral posture with a smile on your face will put dogs into Pack Drive.

These are the body language signals that you need to be aware of:

To put a dog into **Pack Drive**

1 Use a **neutral posture**. Bend *neither* forward nor backwards.

2 Wear a **smile** on your face.

3 Use a **pleasant tone** of voice.

4 **Pet** or touch the dog warmly to elicit Pack Drive.

To put a dog into **Prey Drive**

1 **Lean backwards**, away from your dog.

2 **Wave** or move your **arms.**

3 Use a **high pitch** in your voice.

4 **Run with** your dog.

5 **Throw something** or use food to put a dog into Prey Drive.

Eliciting Pack Drive.

To put a dog into **Defense Drive**

1 **Lean** over or **toward** your dog.

2 Use a **deep** tone of **voice**, not necessarily loud.

3 **Apply collar pressure** or use the leash with pressure.

Knowing how to bring out the Drives in your dog, or knowing what not to do to keep from eliciting certain Drives in your dog, will help you to communicate better with your pets. You will be using these skills while teaching the tricks in this book. Some dogs will need help getting into the correct Drive that they need to be in to learn or perform a particular trick. You can

Eliciting Prey Drive.

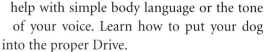

help with simple body language or the tone of your voice. Learn how to put your dog into the proper Drive.

Sometimes your dog will be in the wrong Drive for a particular training session. Knowing how to change to the correct Drive will be very helpful. If your dog is in Pack Drive and you need to switch, just look at the list above and follow those rules. Your dog should be able to switch into the desired Drive.

If your dog is in Prey Drive and needs to be

Eliciting Defense Drive.

in Pack, you must first put your dog into Defense Drive. Prey Drive is very stimulating (active), and dogs need to be brought back into perspective before they can effectively be put into Pack Drive. Pack is an orderly Drive, because pack order is part of that Drive. Follow the rules for Defense Drive, then follow those for Pack Drive, and your dog should be able to be switched into Pack Drive from Prey Drive.

Practice switching your dog's Drives and watch your dog's responses while in each. Notice how your dog's ears are set when in Prey Drive, pricked and listening. Notice how they are in Defense/Flight, back and down. Learn to read your dog and you will learn how to make your dog happy.

Dogs are most *happy* in the Drives that are *high* for them. Dogs are *uncomfortable* if they are in a Drive that is *low* for them. Some tricks need your dog to be in a certain Drive. It is possible to teach a Prey Drive trick in Pack, but you will need to use your imagination and understanding of the Drive in order to do so. Practice and learn. Your imagination is your only limitation.

Couch Potato

This trick has more to it than meets the eye. First of all, a true couch potato

A true coach potato takes natural instinct and born talent.

takes natural instinct and born talent. This is said with some sarcasm, yet it has some validity. *The couch potato trick takes all low Drives; Prey, Pack, Fight, Flight.*

This could be the trick of your dreams. Since being born with low Drives is a natural instinct, not all dogs can be born couch potatoes.

1. Get your dog.

2. Get the remote control.

3. Go to the couch. Lie on one end.

4. Invite your dog to lie on the other end, with the command, "Let's do the Couch Potato trick."

This sounds silly, but the point is that all dogs do something naturally. Find what that thing is, label it, and then teach your dog to do it on command. If your dog gets on the couch without an invitation, teach getting up there on command. If your dog lies under your desk when you sit there, teach going there on command. If your dog begs for food when you eat popcorn in the living room, teach begging on command.

Watch your dog as a professional dog trainer would. See what your dog does *naturally* that you would like to teach to be done on command. Decide what you will call the trick, figure out the command, and then follow the steps as in "Wagging Your Tail."

Read on, this is fun.

When teaching something new, remember to praise while your dog is doing the trick, then release her when finished and give lots and lots of rewards, whether it is hugs and kisses *(Pack Drive)* or food treats *(Prey Drive)*.

Chapter Two

What Every Good Trick Dog Should Know

Picture your dog sitting in the middle of a pile of dog treats on a Stay or quietly laying Down next to a coffee table laden with pizza boxes. These are behaviors every house guest will envy. Imagine your dog waiting for you at the opened gate to your back yard or, while at the park, waiting for you in the back of your van with the hatch wide open. Most passersby will be awed by your amazing dog. These are just a few of the things you can accomplish with what follows in this chapter.

Stay

To Stay means to NOT do anything and get praised for it. To Stay is to hurry up and do nothing. This is an interesting concept for your dog.

Up until now you have been trying to get your dog to do something when given a command. With Stay, you are trying to convey, "When you do *nothing*, What a good sport a Sporting Dog can be!

19

what a good dog you are." At first your dog may think you are crazy for giving praise for nothing. That is why your dog actually has to NOT stay to *learn* STAY. Saying nothing and putting you dog back into position when does not Stay will teach your dog what Stay means.

The sitting position is probably the easiest way to teach the Stay because it is easy to put your dog back into a sitting position by simply lifting the leash over your dog's head and repositioning the dog into the Sit.

Sequence 1. Introduce your dog to the Stay command.

1 On leash, place your dog into a sitting position and praise him for sitting. If you need to help your dog to sit, tuck your arm behind the rear legs and fold the back legs up while gently lifting your dog's collar. Give lots of praise.

2 Tell your dog to "Stay," and give a hand signal for Stay. Use any signal you choose. The most commonly used hand signal would be showing the palm of your hand with the fingers pointing down. During this first step, help by gently holding the leash slightly taut over your dog's head.

3 If your dog moves, say nothing and reposition the Sit. Smile KNOWING that your dog needs to NOT stay in order to learn the Stay.

Show your dog a hand signal for stay and say, "Stay."

4 Relax the leash pressure, praise, and say "OK."

After saying OK, run forward and run with your dog to show that this really is the release and now it's okay to move. There needs to be a clear difference between "Stay" and the release word allowing the dog to move.

Sequence 2. It's time to give your dog a little responsibility.

1 Sit your dog, say "Stay," and show your hand signal.

2 Keep your hands near your waist with *no* pressure on the leash.

Remain close to your dog and hold the leash with nothing swinging loose, *this would be too stimulating for high Prey Drive dogs.* Step in front this time and have the leash in your hand with no pressure over your dog's head.

3 Step back to the side of your dog and praise. Your dog should remain in the Stay while being verbally praised. Your dog should remain until you both run forward after you give the release word.

4 During the Stay, try to walk all the way around your dog. Walk near your dog as you walk around. Gently place your hand on your dog's head as you circle the first time. This first time, your dog will probably try to follow you as you go around. If this happens, just quietly put your dog back into a sitting position, then continue around.

5 If your dog moves from position, take the leash close to the collar and pull up over your dog's head. If necessary, tuck the rear legs back into a Sit. Say nothing until your dog is sitting still again, then smile and praise. Don't forget, your dog needs a big release word to signal that it's okay to move. Silently keep repeating the sitting position, even if the dog stands up, lays Down, or follows you. Remember, this is helping to

Your dog should Stay until given the "OK" release word.

convey the message that you want your dog to do NOTHING. Give a big "OK" release and run forward *with* your dog after you say the release word.

Sequence 3. Gradually increase the time that you expect your dog to Sit and Stay.

1 Sit your dog, say, "Stay," and step out in front of your dog.

2 Remain in front of your dog for 10 seconds at first. Work up to five minutes *gradually*.

When your dog moves on the Sit Stay, take the leash and pull up over your dog's head to repeat the sitting position.

Once off leash, you need to go back and take the collar with both hands to reposition your dog back into sitting position.

3 As long as there is lots of praise and a clear release word (OK), the Stay will become easier and easier. Your dog is not wrong for moving, so say nothing, just put him back into a sit. You are trying to teach your dog to sit still until released.

4 Remember your dog has to NOT Stay and has to be PUT BACK into position in order to learn the Stay.

Sequence 4. Distance

1 Only after the length of time has been increased successfully can you start moving away from your dog a few feet at a time. Start with three feet on leash.

2 If that is successful, move to six feet on leash the next time.

3 Eventually take the leash off and practice putting your dog back into a sitting position *without* the use of the leash. When your dog gets up, slowly go back to the dog and tuck him into a Sit using the collar and a little rear leg tuck if necessary.

4 Remain at six feet off leash for a while until your dog is really solid on the command Stay. Also, your dog will need practice being put back without the use of the leash so that when you do get to greater distances, your dog will not leave as you approach to put him back into the sitting position should he move.

5 Get farther and farther away, but only increase your distance by two feet at a time.

Sequence 5. Distractions

1 After you can do a six-foot Sit Stay with no leash for five minutes, it is time to start doing Stays around distractions. Take your dog to the corner store and practice out front while people are going in and out.

2 Go the park during a sports event.

3 Have your own sports event and throw balls and toys around while your dog is on the Stay.

4 Remember, each time your dog moves from position, silently go back and reposition the Sit. The slower you move around your dog on a Sit-Stay, the more chance you have for success. *Remember the Prey Drive is stimulated by lots of motion.* Your arms, your hair, your neck tie, or your leash can all swing too much and make it difficult for your dog to Stay. Help your dog to be successful.

Take your dog to the shopping center and practice while people are going in and out.

The Stay Trick Challenge

Here is where the Stays really become FUN. *Stays are Pack Drive behaviors.* When you add the challenge, you test your dog's knowledge of the Stay command. When you use a Prey Drive challenge: food, toy, or motion, you will be stimulating your dog's Prey Drive.

Be ready for what may happen. Your dog might move on the Stay command. You will need to react immediately, but move *slowly* around your dog. Don't use a Defensive challenge such as loud noises, or something coming toward your dog. It isn't fair, and if your dog has much Flight Drive, it will cause too much stress. You can even use a Pack Drive challenge. Have someone come up and talk to or even pet your dog while on the Stay command. If your dog is high in Pack Drive, you might get lots of tail wagging or even a jump up. Be ready to put your dog back into position. Have fun with this.

Challenge your dog on the Stay:

1. Give the "Stay" command and toss a piece of food on the ground in front of your dog. Remember, your dog must Stay or be put back.

2. Make sure *you*, (not the dog) get the food if the Stay is broken by the dog going for it.

3. Reset the Stay position, say nothing, and throw the food again.

4. If you see no movement when the food is tossed, signal the release and let your dog have the goodie. *This is a real challenge. Don't try this unless you have done all the preliminary work leading up to it.* To be fair to your dog, your dog needs to understand the word "Stay" before you try the food challenge. Have fun with the Stay command. It can be a trick in itself.

Challenge your dog on Stays once the command is understood.

5 Ask a bystander, "Can you do something distracting so I can see if my dog would break the Stay?" Be fair and work up to the big distractions, like kids, bikes, and Frisbees. Practice makes perfect.

6 Always remember to give a big release and let your dog have the distraction—if possible—or a food reward in its place. Always give lots of love with your releases.

Leadership Exercises

Respect is a very important concept when working with your dog. You must respect your dog and your dog must respect you. Your responsibility lies in treating your dog with fairness and kindness.

Learning something new can be very confusing at first, that is until your dog understands and the light bulb goes on. Until then, you must take everything step by step. Show the dog exactly what you want and praise lavishly even though *you* did all of the work. You placed, moved, and helped the dog and *she* gets all the glory. Praise and clap your hands, yippee with glee, and give a treat when your dog does well or tries hard. Dogs love these training sessions and the time you spend together. Your dog will start to try harder and harder to beat you to the punch, and before long she will be doing all the work and *you* can sit back and take in all the applause.

$E = MC^2$

$Excellence = Mutual\ Caring^2$

Respect is a very important concept when working with your dog.

Your dog's responsibility, as far as respect goes, is to learn to work *for you. The difference between working for someone and working with someone is simple: the* leader *makes up the rules of the game.* You decide when you are going to play and for how long. You own the ball and you are going to let your dog play with it—but it's *your game.* You will play fair, and you will have fun, but, simply said, *you* are the coach and your dog is the player. As I said before, respect travels both ways, from you to your dog and from your dog to you. If you have ever been coached, you know that you work a lot harder for someone you respect than someone you don't. You don't need to be tough, just clear and consistent.

You need to show your dog what leadership is. The best way to do that is a simple sequence of exercises called the Long Sit and the Long Down. These exercises are simple to do. All you will need is your dog, a timepiece, and a smile. Let's start with the Long Down.

The Long Down

Sequence 1. This should be done three times before going to Sequence 2.

1. Sit on the floor and place your dog into a Down position next to you. Praise quietly, but do not release the dog from the Down position. Keep your hands off during this exercise *except* to put the dog back into a Down position.

2. Start timing for 30 minutes. Don't panic, see the important note at the end of the list. It is a good idea to use a half hour comedy TV show to keep some levity in your attitude.

3. Every time your dog gets up put her back into the Down position. Take your hands off once your dog is Down, even if only for a few seconds.

4. If your dog pushes against you, move away slightly. Stay on the floor nearby so that you are close enough to put the dog back Down immediately.

5. Keep chew toys and food away during a Long Down, as these articles would keep your dog in the Down position, not the dog's desire to please you. Instead it is you, the coach, who is keeping the dog in Down position. Each time you reposition

your dog, it is not necessary to repeat the Down command. Just put the dog back. Smile to yourself knowing what a learning opportunity this is becoming.

6 After 30 minutes, praise and give a BIG RELEASE. Say, "OK," and make your dog get up and move. If she fell asleep, wake her up for the release.

Long Downs are successful only if you put your dog back each time the dog gets up.

7 Do this three times during the next few days.

Important Note: To be successful at this leadership exercise, your dog does not need to be perfectly still while in the Down position for the full 30 minutes. To be successful, *every time your dog does get up, you need to put her back into the Down position.* Then you would be having a *successful* training session. You can do it; you just need to be clear to your dog what you want, and that is to remain next to you in a Down position for the amount of time *you* determine.

Sequence 2. This step should be done three times before moving to Sequence 3.

1 Sit in a chair next to your dog in the Down position. This elevates your posture and distances you slightly from the dog. It teaches that you can still maintain control from a chair a few inches away.

2 Time this Long Down for 30 minutes also. Then release after the time is up. The same rules apply as in sequence one; always put your dog back into the Down if your dog should move or get up.

3 It is advisable to distract your-self during these sessions. You might want to watch a half hour TV show. When the show starts, Down your dog. When the show ends, release your dog. TV can help you pass the time. But don't get so distracted that you forget about your number one player, your dog. Keep an eye out, so you can repo-sition the dog when necessary.

4 Do this three times over the course of a few days. On alternate days do the Long Sit. (See below for Long Sit.)

Elevate your position by sitting in a chair.

Sequence 3. Follow the same steps seen in Sequence 2, except that now you are in a chair a few feet away.

1 Put your dog in a Down position and then go sit down yourself.

2 As before, get up and reposition into the Down position if your dog should move.

3 Increase the distance between you and your dog to 8–10 feet over the next three sessions.

4 Release after 30 minutes.

5 Again do this sequence three times, alternating with the Long Sit.

Sequence 4. This should be done at least three times, and repeated any time you need a little extra control in your relationship with your dog.

1 As in Sequence 3, after your dog is in a Down position, sit in a chair.

2 But don't stay put in your chair the entire time. Move around the room occasionally. Get up and change the channel on the TV instead or go look out the window. Get up and move to another chair. Don't leave your dog's field of vision, however.

3 After 30 minutes give the release and get your dog up with a big "OK."

4 Do this step three times and repeat as needed for control if the dog gets too keyed up.

The Long Sit

Move around the room during a Long Down.

The Long Sit is the same as the Long Down, except your dog is in a sitting position, and it is only done for 10 minutes. The Sit is a little less comfortable, so it is done for a shorter time period. Follow the different levels as for the Down.

Dogs who have had no trouble remaining in a Down will probably lie down during the Long Sit. This will therefore give you the opportunity of reinforcing the Sit, since showing the dog that you make the decisions is part of this exercise. You *need* to reinforce the position if your dog has moved.

1 Start with a 10 minute session with you in a chair next to your sitting dog. Do this three times on alternating days with the Long Down.

2 The next step is to do a 10 minute session with you a short distance from your sitting dog. Do this three times on alternating days with the Long Down.

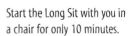

Start the Long Sit with you in a chair for only 10 minutes.

3 Finally, do a 10 minute Sit with you moving around the room in full view of your dog. Do three times on days alternating with the Long Down.

Remember, the success of these exercises lies in the length of time they are done, and in the fact that you will always replace your dog when he gets up or changes position.

Either the Long Sit or the Long Down will be more challenging for your dog. Do most frequently the one that requires more participation from you. Remember that the act of putting your dog back is the leadership element to these exercises. It is time well spent. Ten minute Sits and 30 minute Downs are like the coach telling the team to do 50 push ups and 20 laps around the gym.

Take Me Out to the Ball Game: The Retrieve

If your dog is a natural retriever, you are in luck. Not all dogs instinctively carry things in their mouths. Even if they do, they may not always want to give those things to you. Chasing a moving article through the air doesn't light up every dog's life. *A dog with low Prey Drive will be harder to motivate into retrieving something than a dog with high Prey Drive.* A dog with high Prey *and* Pack Drives will not only want to go get the toy, but will bring it *back to you too.*

Wherever your dog falls on the Prey Drive scale, she can be taught to retrieve. It may take a little longer, but with the help of some alternative methods, it can and should be done. A lot of tricks requires dogs to hold something in their mouths. Even if your dog doesn't have to get the item, holding it is a part of retrieving. Giving it back is also a big part. Let's look at each part.

Chase the item.

Pick it up.

Hold the item.

Carry it.

Coming back to you with the item.

You can get your dog to retrieve anything.

Giving it back when you ask for it.

Where to Start

The Volhard Motivational Retrieve is a step-by-step approach that will result in a solid retriever. Pick something that you want your dog to fetch, maybe a stick, a ball, a dumbbell, or a piece of old leather.

Gently open your dog's mouth and place the stick in position.

1. **Start with** some **treats** and offer one to your dog saying "Take it," as she takes the treat from your fingers. You can offer the food on a spoon that will help associate metal with retrieving. This will help if you ever want your dog to pick up something metal, like car keys or dropped silverware. Tell your dog to, "Take it," 10 times and stop. Do it again ten times until your dog's mouth opens anxiously when you say, "Take it."

2. **Select something** for your dog to retrieve. Here we will use a stick. Take your stick in one hand and gently open your dog's mouth with the other hand by putting your finger behind the canine tooth.

   Say "Take it," gently place the stick into your dog's mouth, and cup the mouth shut for two seconds while you smile and praise your dog. Exchange the stick for a treat while saying, "Give." Really pet your dog between tries. Do this step 10 times and take a break. Go for a short walk or play something else for a minute or so, then do 10 more. Do this step five times until your dog willingly holds the stick for just a few seconds while you gently hold her mouth closed praising. Always exchange the stick for a treat.

3 Say, "**Take it,**" offer the stick just in front of your dog's nose, tickling her lip with it. Have your dog next to you on the left, holding the collar with two fingers of your left hand while tickling your dog's nose with the stick in your right hand. If your dog takes it, let go of the collar and cup her mouth shut as you did in the last step. Then praise and smile.

After just a couple of seconds, exchange the stick for a treat. If your dog shows any sign of thinking about taking the stick, place it in your dog's mouth and cup the mouth shut. Praise your dog and exchange the stick for food with the "Give" command. Some signs that your dog is thinking about retrieving are:

- 🐾 staring at the stick,

- 🐾 licking her own nose or lips,

- 🐾 or bumping the stick with her nose.

If you see any of these signs, put the stick in your dog's mouth as if she had taken it herself. Do this step only as long as it takes for your dog to voluntarily take the stick.

4 Once your dog willingly takes the stick, you need to teach holding it. Go back to placing it in the dog's mouth and cupping her mouth shut. Praise her. Slowly bring your hand under your dog's mouth and help lift your dog's muzzle into a natural position for carrying the stick.

Smile and praise—it means a lot to your dog to see you smile. Tell your dog "Hold it." Lower your hand slightly and repeat "Hold it." Gently lift the muzzle again if

Cup your dog's mouth shut after positioning the stick.

the dog starts to roll the stick around in her mouth or isn't holding it firmly. Say, "Hold it." After just five seconds the first time, say, "Give," and remove the stick from her mouth. Remember to exchange it for a treat and give lots of praise between each hold.

Never let your dog drop the item into your hands or onto the floor. Work up to 30 seconds for holding it, five seconds at a time. If your dog drops the stick, be more enthusiastic about lifting her muzzle with a little tap under the jaw. *Remember your dog's Drives. With high Flight Drive, just lifting the muzzle will be enough.*

5 Reaching for the stick is the next step. With your dog on your left, slide two fingers into the collar. With the right hand about two inches in front of your dog's nose, offer the stick and say, "Take it." If the dog reaches for it, cup her mouth shut and lay on the praise. Exchange for food and do a dance.

If your dog doesn't offer to take the stick, keep it just in front of her nose. Move the stick with your dog's nose. As a correction, slightly twist the collar to tighten it a little. Teach your dog to hold the stick. Hold the pressure for *only a few seconds* if your dog has much Flight Drive. *If she has plenty of Fight Drive, hold it for no more than 20 seconds.*

Watch for any signs that the dog is thinking about taking the stick, as you did earlier. If you see any sign at all, or think you do, *relax* the collar and put the stick into your dog's mouth. Praise *heavily* as though it was the dog's idea to take the stick.

After the pressure, put the stick in your dog's mouth even if she didn't take it. *Exchange the stick for food and try again.* Keep trying until your dog truly does take the stick. The key here is to make the exchange lots of fun with nothing other than smiles and praise. Your dog needs to enjoy training sessions and so do you. Take breaks after every few repetitions.

6 Once your dog holds the stick and reaches for it alone, you need to teach holding the stick while walking. Place the stick in the dog's mouth, say "Hold it" and "Let's go." Gently help your dog to walk as you lift her muzzle up into a natural position. *Take only a few steps at a time and* then *exchange the stick for food.* If the stick gets dropped, just stop there and do a 30 second stick hold right where you are. Try to get your dog to walk while holding the stick. Lots of praise and enthusiasm helps teach your dog that she is doing the right thing. Remember, lots and lots of praise.

7 Once your dog can walk while holding the stick, you are just one step away from true retrieving. Your dog must be able to pick-up the stick from the ground. Try to get your dog to take the stick while walking, as you keep the stick just a few inches in front of her nose.

Move with your dog and present the stick just in front of her for a moving retrieve. Move along with your dog and say, "Take it." After each moving retrieve, exchange the stick for food and then praise. Gradually lower the stick as you move along. Get your dog to lower her head and grab for the stick. Give lots of praise and reward. Make it as much fun as you can. Finally, put one end of the stick on the floor and hold the other end up on an angle. Tell your dog to take it. Wow, *give lots of praise.* If your dog needs to be reminded, use just a little collar pressure to move her toward the stick and help her pick it up. *The more help your dog needs, the more praise should be given.*

If your dog loses interest, you have either played too long or haven't made it fun enough for your dog. *Remember her Drives.* Lots of activity is fun for dogs with lots of Prey Drive. Lots of petting, smiles, and hugs is fun for dogs with lots of Pack. Make the stick the prize for dogs with lots of Fight Drive. *You need to know what motivates your dog and utilize it.*

8 Once your dog picks up the object from the ground, you are ready.

Throw the stick and send your dog at the same time. This is called a live retrieve and is usually very motivating. Call your dog back to you as she picks up the stick. After this becomes routine, it

Gently lift the muzzle if your dog stops having a firm grip on the stick.

Teach your dog to walk while holding the stick.

Your dog must be able to pick the stick up from the ground.

shouldn't be necessary to actually call the dog during a retrieve. The dog should automatically bring the item back to you.

Remember, reward the dog for each retrieve. For some dogs, just throwing the toy again is a reward. Others will require something more. *You* will know what it takes to let your dog know she is a star in your eyes.

Throw the stick and send your dog at the same time.

Your dog should not go after something you have thrown until told to "Take it."

9 Finally you can put the Stay (*See* Page 21) together with the Retrieve. Your dog should not go after something you have thrown until you say to get it.

If you have practiced the Stay Challenge, this will be very easy. Tell your dog to Stay and then throw a toy. Wait a second and then tell your dog to "Take it." After all of your training, your dog should fly out to the item, pick it up, and bring it directly to you. What a good dog! If all does not go as planned, it is time for a little review, and that is okay.

It is never a problem to review your training. It is all part of working and playing with a dog. Remember, repetition, along with fun and consistency, is part of the whole picture. Keep up the good work.

Read on, I can't wait to see what's next.

Chapter THREE

Practical Tricks

Tricks fall into categories ranging from entertaining to handy. Here are some practical, useful tricks that will not only impress, but might aid you in your daily tasks and "living with" your dog.

Door Manners (The Invisible Door)

Having a dog with door manners may be your best trick yet. The trick is teaching your dog never to cross a threshold without permission. Some examples of the thresholds (invisible doors) you will want to teach are the front door, the back door, the gate to your fenced yard, the car door, the basement door, and the top of the stairs. The list can be endless.

Not only will this trick amaze your friends, it will be the most practical thing that you will teach your dog. Imagine someone leaving the gate to your back yard ajar and your dog staying in the yard. Imagine your dog never trying to run out the front door unattended or staying in the car while you load and unload parcels you

A group of Terriers.

are carrying. Imagine your dog waiting at the top of the stairs instead of getting underfoot and tripping you.

It really is simple. With just a few training sessions you will be wondering how you *ever* could have lived with your dog without door manners.

Pack Drive is necessary because it requires maximum cooperation from your dog. Some Defense/Fight Drive is helpful for this trick. Make this trick enjoyable with lots of *fun releases*, and it will be possible for almost any dog.

Sequence 1. Put your dog on leash for a training session at the front door of your house or apartment.

The commands you will use are: "Wait" and "OK." "*Wait*" will signal your dog *not to cross* the threshold. "*OK*" will signal permission to cross the threshold. Obviously, you will not always use "OK" because sometimes your dog will not be leaving with you. For those times, you will be free to leave home without your dog following at your heels or bolting out the door.

Start by walking up to the door with your dog on leash and then opening the door. Make sure the leash is loose and you are not pulling or holding your dog back. Open the door as you say "Wait." Then, the instant your dog starts to cross the threshold, quickly pull on the leash to bring your dog back in. Close the door and try again. Act as if you had nothing to do with

When visitors come by, your dog won't cross over the threshold.

your dog's being pulled back into the room. There you are just smiling and saying, "What a good dog!" Your dog thinks, "Hmm, it must have been the *threshold* that pulled me back, my *owner* is fine and happy. I think I'll stay on this side with my owner." Remember:

1 **Open** the door with your dog on a **loose** leash.

2 **Say,** "Wait."

3 **Pull back** quickly on the leash if the dog's foot starts to cross the threshhold.

4 Let the **door close** with both of you still inside.

5 **Act** as if you had nothing to do with the pull back. Praise your dog.

6 **Repeat** until your dog starts to hesitate crossing the threshold.

Sequence 2. Repeat step one, but instead of closing the door, hesitate and say, "OK" and let your dog cross over the threshold. This should help make it clear for the dog not to move until permission is given.

1 **Open** the door and **say,** "Wait."

2 **Pull back** if your dog should start to cross.

3 **Say "OK,"** and let your dog cross.

From here on, you can never allow your dog to go through the front door without you saying, "OK," even when you are just going for a walk *with* your dog. You need to be consistent. Remind yourself with a note taped to the door frame. Simply say, "OK" *when* you and your dog go outside *together*.

It is a good idea for reinforcing your leadership that you cross all thresholds first, but that is up to you and your relationship with your dog. Just remember that

After waiting at the threshold for a few seconds, say, "OK" and let your dog cross over with you.

your dog is being taught to never cross the opening without hearing "OK." You want and need to be consistent so your dog will learn quickly and understand. Be clear and fair to your dog. Be consistent.

Sequence 3. This time *you are* going through the door and the *dog is not*. Remember, always approach the door with a loose leash—don't *hold* your dog back. If your dog tries to cross, quickly pull back.

Next, you need to step just outside and pull the leash back into the house if your dog tries to follow. You will do this by extending your arm *back into* the doorway, pulling the leash around the door. Open the door and be ready to pull the leash back in the house if your dog tries to join you on the outside. Then say, "OK" and let your dog join you with lots of praise.

1. **Open** the door with your dog on a loose leash.

2. Say, "Wait."

3. **Pull back** on the leash before the dog's foot crosses the opening.

4. **Go out,** but extend your arm through the door, pulling back if your dog follows. **Let the door close** on the leash.

5. **Open** the **door** and keep your dog from coming out toward you.

6. Say, **"OK"** and let your dog come to you.

7. Give lots and lots of praise.

While you are on the other side of the threshold from your dog, reach back in to put your dog back if he starts to cross over.

**Sequence 4. Do Sequences 1 through 3
coming *back into* the house.**

Sequence 5. Take the leash off.

Walk up to the door with your dog and say, "Wait." When you open the
door, be ready to pull the door back quickly if a nose starts to go out.
Don't actually close the door on the nose, just have the door coming
closer to make an impression on your dog. Start to open the door again,
close the door quickly and pull back on your dog's collar to remind
your dog not to cross. Open the door and go through yourself. Keeping
the door open, look back at your dog and say, "OK," and let your dog
come with you with lots and lots of praise.

If you have more than one dog, teach each one separately.

1. **Open** the door with your dog off leash.

2. **Say, "Wait."**

3. **Before** the dog's foot crosses the opening, **pull back quickly** on the door and/or the dog's collar.

4. **Open the door** and go out alone.

5. **Say, "OK"** and welcome your dog through.

Sequence 6. Start all over with other doors and openings.

Start with sequence 1 at the backyard gate and go all the way through sequence five. Then start with sequence one again for your car doors and go all the way through sequence five. Practice at any opening your dog should not cross without permission.

Sequence 7. If you have more than one dog, train one dog at a time so each has an opportunity to learn door manners alone.

After they have all learned and mastered door manners, you should be able to handle the group at the door—with no leashes—and allow only the one dog you call to cross the threshold to be with you. Practice makes perfect.

Nothing will impress your friends more when they come to visit.

Go Ahead, Make My Day

You can even teach your dog not to cross a chalk line on the floor or in the dirt in the same manner. Just draw the line and take your dog through sequences one through five, using the line as a threshold. You can teach that dog of yours anything you want.

You can do old western movie remakes. Draw the line on the floor and say, "OK, go ahead. I dare you to cross this line." Your dog will cross over because you said, "OK." Then look nervous and draw another line and say, "Well, how about this line? Go ahead, OK, go ahead." Then do it *one more time* and really start to sweat. Draw a line and say, "I dare you to cross THIS line.

"OK, I dare you to cross this line."

Go ahead, what's stopping you, go ahead . . . *OK.*" When your dog *does* cross it, run for the hills and get your *dog* to *chase you.* You should get an academy award for that one.

Stair Manners

How many times have you competed with your dog for the right of way on the stairs? This can be very dangerous for both you and your dog, not to mention guests. Teaching your dog that going up and down stairs is a solo act is not only wise, it is safety rule number two. Door manners is safety rule number one.

Just as with doors, set up training sessions on the stairs in your house. With your dog on leash, approach the top of the stairs and say, "Wait," and start down the steps. If your dog follows, pull back on the leash to put him back at the top of the stairs. Start down the stairs again. If the stairs are long, leave the leash draped on the steps. *Go back, take the leash, and begin again if your dog follows you.* Stair Masters have nothing on stair manners. You may be going back up the stairs each time you get to the bottom if your dog follows you before you have

For safety and fun, teach stair manners too.

said, "OK." When you finally get to the bottom, turn and face your dog saying, "OK." *Remember to give lots of praise when your dog gets to you.*

Teach door manners before stair manners so your dog understands what "Wait" means, unless you want the exercise running up and down the stairs to begin again when your dog follows you.

Clean Up Your Room *or* Pick Up Your Laundry

Everybody in the household should be responsible for his or her own mess and should clean it up willingly. Some of us have more chores than others, but even the smallest members of the family need to pull their own weight.

Your dog is no different. With free room and board comes your dogs picking up their own toys! Of course, this means you will have to buy your dog a lot of new toys and an appropriate toy chest. I don't think you will get any objections from your dogs on this point.

Prey Drive is what makes dogs want to play with most toys, especially squeaky toys and flying, floppy toys. Soft cloth toys can be Prey Drive toys too, unless your dog mothers them, then they are Pack Drive toys. Make sure you get your dog's favorite types so that playing with them becomes fun for both you and your dog. The toy chest you use should be size appropriate for your dog to allow your dog to drop the toys into it.

Step 1. You will need to teach your dog to **retrieve** with the sequences in "Take Me Out to the Ball Game: The Retrieve" (*See* page 32). You need to have a reliable *fetch command* in order for your dog to pick up all the toys and ultimately put them all away. After you have mastered the "Take It" command, and your dog is bringing the wanted items to you, you are ready to move on.

Step 2. Next, teach your dog to pick up different things from around the room—on *your commands.* The steps for teaching this is in the trick "Find What I Have Lost" (page 56). If your dog's ball is in the middle of the living room floor, when you point to it and say, "Take your ball," will your dog bring it to you? If not, work on getting your dog to retrieve different toys for you as you take the toys and then ask for another toy. Label the toys by name as in "Find

With your dog's free room and board comes picking up the toys.

What I Have Lost." Remember to reward your dog for each toy brought to you. In the retrieving tricks, throwing the item again is part of the reward.

With this trick, the item is not thrown again, therefore you must praise your dog adequately for giving the item to you. During the learning process, *use each toy* and play with your dog for a few minutes before asking for another toy. Put each toy away and ask for another. This will be more fun for your dog than immediately giving up each item.

Start with a pile of toys on the floor. Ask your dog to bring you a toy. Play with it for a few seconds and say, "Give." Take the toy, release your dog, and give a treat. Put the toy in the box yourself, and then ask for another toy to be brought to you. Point to the pile and ask for the next toy. Repeat the process until all of the toys have been brought to you and then have been put away.

End the training session playing with a favorite toy and permitting your dog to keep it. If you ask for the toys, put them away, and then ignore the dog with no toys, your dog will quickly learn not to participate in this trick. Why should he, he ends up with no toys and no fun.

So, as always, look at the trick from your dog's point of view. See how bringing all the toys, one by one, ends with getting to keep the best one and getting to play with all of them along the way.

Step 3. Now it is time to teach your dog to "Drop" the toy in the box rather than to "Give" it to you. Gather up some toys and get the toy box yourself.

Give your dog a toy rather than having him pick one up. This way you are working on pieces of the trick one at a time. Now you are working on dropping the toy into the box, therefore *do not* work on the retrieving or the identification part. Have the toy box right next to you and tell your dog to "Put it away." Offer your hand over the box, and if your dog drops the toy, move your hand and let the toy go directly into the box. Give lots of praise. Reward either with a treat or by playing with the put-away toy.

If your dog doesn't offer you the toy, gently remove it by opening your dog's mouth with mild pressure from above on the lips over your dog's teeth. If you press lightly with your dog's lips over the upper teeth, the mouth should open. Give tremendous praise for dropping the item into the box. Toss it out of the box and let your dog play with it again as a reward. Stop after you have had any amount of success with this. Do not over practice this at one time. You should always end each training session on a fun note.

Step 4. Practice the "Put it away" command daily. Offer your dog a toy right next to the box. Say, "Put it away." Help him drop it into the box with lots of praise and play. Make dropping the toy into the box the game. The easier it is for your dog, the more fun it becomes because you are making it a game.

Work on this until you no longer need to help your dog drop the toy into the box. When you can offer him a toy a few feet away from the box, command "Put it away," and your dog walks to the box and drops it in, you are then ready to start putting steps together.

Step 5. Combine Step 2 and Step 4. Have a couple of toys near the box. Ask your dog to "Get" a particular toy. Now tell your dog to "Put it away." Help guide your dog to the box. Tap the edge and point into it. Remember to help your dog be successful when necessary. When the toy is in the box, praise and praise your dog, give the release word *and* a treat. This is not only great fun for your dog, but will help you too.

Step 6. Now you are ready for your dog to do the pick-up chores. Scatter several toys around the room. Place the toy box in an easily accessible spot in the same room. Command your dog to "Get" a toy, and then command your dog to "Put it away." At this point it should not be necessary to help, but it is better to review than to get frustrated if your dog is having trouble. *Patience* is what training is all about.

Step 7. You can teach picking up any item that your dog is trained to retrieve. Use your imagination on how you can impress house guests with this trick.

Practice by using cloth napkins at the coffee table. Keep a laundry basket nearby and have your dog help you clean up after the guests have finished eating. Or use paper napkins and have your dog throw them in the trash basket. If your guests have taken their shoes off, have your dog place them in the shoe basket. Remember, let your imagination be your limitation.

Go Find Daddy *or*
Wake Up the Kids *or*
Take This to Grandma

Sending your dog through the house to find someone can save your legs and your mind. Trying to wake up kids in the morning can become a breeze with the help of the family dog. Finding the lost hobbyist in the bowels of the basement or attic is no longer impossible when you have a friend with four on the floor. Waiting on guests is far more entertaining when you have someone with floppy ears to help out, so why do it alone? Teach your dog to become your sidekick for all of these daily tasks.

Dogs can carry things such as notes or requests in their mouths. Dogs can jump up on beds to wake up impossible sleepers. Dogs can transport items tied to their collars like a butler with a tray to the far reaches of your house.

With a few simple steps you can make this practical and fun trick into one of the best uses for your dog's abilities. After all, everyone deserves to earn their keep. This trick has elements of Pack, Prey, and Defense Drive in it. Pack Drive comes in finding another pack member, Prey in running and carrying, and Defense/Fight Drive in having the confidence to leave the room alone.

Step 1. Start with one other person in the household. Decide on the names that your dog will know you by. For example, when your dogs *are* the kids in the family, the adults can be mommy and daddy. So the commands can be "Go find Daddy" and "Go find Mommy." When there are more than two people in the household, proper names can be used, but start teaching this trick with just two of you. First your dog needs to learn to find *one other* person *before* being able to discriminate between different people in the house.

Step 2. Get your dog, some treats, the person to be found, and a long leash or line.

You and your partner need to kneel about six feet apart from each other, with your dog on leash. One person has the end of the leash and the other person has the dog by the collar. The person with the dog gives the command, "Go find Daddy" and releases the dog. "Daddy," the person with the leash, helps guide the dog towards him, *leaning backwards on his heels to keep from leaning foreward and putting the dog into Defense Drive.* When the dog arrives, "Daddy" offers a small treat taking the dog gently by the collar and praising the dog. He should make the experience very pleasant and fun for the dog. After all, your dog has found "Daddy" and that's wonderful.

Go find Daddy, Mommy, Sister, etc.

While "Daddy" is praising the dog, he needs to toss the end of the leash back to you. Do this back and forth several times, the full length of the leash, until your dog is flying between the two of you, always of course waiting for the command, "Go find so and so." Change the length of time between commands. By making the times random between calls, you will be teaching your dog to learn the command, "Go find someone," rather than teaching your dog to just run back and forth between you.

- Have your dog on leash.
- Two people kneel facing each other the same distance as the leash is long.
- One person holds the leash, the other holds the dog.
- The person with the dog says, "Go find so and so."
- The leash holder helps guide the dog to him or her.
- The same person holds the collar, feeds the dog, and praises.
- Switch roles with you partner.

Step 3. Take the leash off and increase the distance between the two people by only a few feet. Repeat as in step two, but this time, *don't use the leash.* If your dog doesn't go to your partner directly, then it is your job to silently take the dog's collar and walk to the indicated person. When your dog gets there, even if with human assistance, the "found person" should really lay on the praise. Make your dog really want to find that person the next time.

If your dog needs help too many times in a row, simply put the leash back on and continue with step two. If you are successful, gradually increase the distance between the two people. Try to stay in sight of each other.

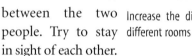
Increase the distance between two people until they are in different rooms

Remember to hold your dog until you send him, and help your dog (if necessary) without giving another command.

- 🐾 Have your dog off leash.

- 🐾 Two people kneel, facing each other a short distance apart.

- 🐾 One person holds the dog.

- 🐾 The person with the dog says, "Go find so and so," and lets go of the dog. When the dog finds the person indicated, that person takes hold of the collar, feeds the dog, and praises.

- 🐾 If the dog doesn't go, the sender takes the dog to the hunted person. Praise just the same.

- 🐾 Switch roles.

Step 4. Now that your dog is doing the finding without a leash, gradually go out of sight of each other. First go just around the corner, then to another room down the hall. Eventually go upstairs and downstairs.

It is very important to change the length of time between commands. You want your dog to perform *on command*, not just to run between the two of you, grabbing the treat, and running back again. Take hold of your dog's collar and praise with a treat reward. Then wait and send your dog back on command.

- 🐾 Have your dog off leash.
- 🐾 Two people kneel out of sight of one another.
- 🐾 The person with the dog says, "Go find so and so," and lets the dog go.
- 🐾 When the dog finds the person indicated, that person takes hold of the collar, feeds, and praises the dog.
- 🐾 If the dog doesn't go, the sender leads the dog to the hunted person. Praise just the same.
- 🐾 Reverse roles.

Step 5. At the beginning of each training session, you need to go back to the previous step for review. Practice these steps until your dog has no trouble finding you or your partner.

After many training sessions, try sending your dog to find your partner *without* a review step. Cue your partner about your plan and go to another part of the house. After a few minutes, command your dog, "Go find Daddy." Remember, be ready to help your dog, but don't repeat your command over and over again. If your dog goes right to the job at hand and finds your partner, make sure that the found person really gives lots of praise to your dog. This is really wonderful and deserves great rewards.

- 🐾 Without a review, but with a plan, send your dog to find someone.
- 🐾 When your dog finds the person indicated, that person takes hold of the collar, feeds the dog, and praises a lot.
- 🐾 If the dog doesn't go, the sender takes the dog to the hunted person. Praise just the same.

Step 6. After much success with Step 5, it is time to teach your dog to tell the difference between family members. Start with everybody in a circle and repeat Step 2 by using the leash again. Toss the leash to Sally and command, "Go find Sally." Let her praise and reward and then toss the leash to someone else. She then commands, "Go find Mommy." Continue until you have named everyone, and your dog is having a great time waiting for the "Go find so and so" command and finding that particular person.

- Get into a circle of people, with your dog on leash.
- One person holds the leash, another holds the dog.
- The person with the dog says, "Go find so and so."
- The leash holder helps guide the dog to him/her.
- The same person holds the collar, feeds the dog, and praises.
- Continue until everyone is named. Give lots of praise to your dog.

Step 7. Spread your circle out and take your dog off leash. Continue as in Step 6 and randomly send your dog to all the members of your circle. The sender quietly helps the dog find the right person each time, if necessary.

Make sure that your body posture is not putting your dog into Defense Drive by towering over or dragging your dog. The found person must also look very welcoming, kneeling back on his or her heels, and allowing your dog to come quickly and happily.

- Get into a circle of people, with your dog off leash.
- The person with the dog says, "Go find so and so."
- The found person takes hold of the collar and feeds the dog.
- Continue until everyone is named. Give lots of praise to your dog.

Step 8. As in Step 4, go out of sight and into different rooms of the house until your dog is running through the house *finding all* the members participating in the training session. It is not necessary to have all members of the family work on this step every time you practice. But do review the previous step when you start up each training session.

Step 9. As in Step 5, plan with one member of the household that you are going to send your dog—cold turkey—to find him/her. Go into another room and wait for a while, then send your dog on the mission. Remember to be ready to help your dog if necessary.

It is these helping sessions that really make what you want clear to your dog. Don't ever lose your patience, but rather quietly take your dog to the missing person. Even with your help, your dog must always get praised as if performing without help.

- Without a review, but with a plan, send your dog to find someone.

- When your dog finds the person indicated, that person takes hold of the collar, feeds the dog, and praises a lot.

- If your dog doesn't go, the sender leads the dog to the hunted person. Praise just the same.

Step 10. Your imagination is your only limitation as to how you can best use this trick. You can get a pouch for your dog's collar with a bell on it to signal the person that a note has arrived, or a back pack for your dog to carry bigger things to the other parts of the house. If your dog will carry something, (see retrieving chapter) then you can have him deliver, first hand (or should we say, first mouth) the intended item for the lost family member.

When did you hire a butler? Wow, it's Rover.

NOTE: This is not recommended for sandwich delivery unless the other person is on a diet. Have fun.

The "Living Vacuum"

How many times have you dropped something while cooking? What do you do with food once it has hit the floor? Certainly, you can't use it. Plus you have to stop and bend over to pick it up. What you need is a vacuum that is always available on an instant's notice, that doesn't run out of battery power or have long cords to deal with. Sounds like one where your dog can come to the rescue. *Dogs with a fair amount of Prey Drive will do this trick naturally.* The vacuum trick is an easy one to teach.

Step 1. Get several pieces of something edible. Start in the kitchen or eating area of your home. Casually drop a piece of food, point to it with your toe, and say, "Vacuum." Tap the floor with your toe *rather than* pointing with your finger. You want your dog to look down at the floor, not up at your hands. If necessary, place your hands out of sight as you tap the floor with your toe. Praise when your dog finds the food and eats it. Release with a big "OK."

A four-legged vacuum is available on an instant's notice.

Step 2. Do not necessarily drop the bits of treat in full view of your dog. Distract your dog or have someone else distract him, drop something and command, "Vacuum." When your dog automatically looks down at hearing "Vacuum," you have taught the trick. Praise while your dog is looking for the tidbit and release after it has been eaten.

Step 3. Reinforce this trick on a regular basis. Do not let too many days go by without practicing. If you are a clumsy chef or have kids who toss things at the table, your dog will be a pro in no time!

The trick teaches your dog to hunt for something on the floor on the "Vacuum" command. Have fun; your dog will.

Find What I Have Lost

How many times a week do you hunt for your misplaced keys, or worse, the lost remote control? Lost items can make you crazy. What better trick, then, could there be than teaching your dog to find what you have lost? *Having a dog with a good nose for scent is part of Prey Drive. Finding the lost item and bringing it back to you is part of Pack Drive. Since this trick takes both Drives, your dog will need some of each.*

Step 1. First, you need to teach your dog to find something in particular and bring it to you. Take your pick of items, but keep the following in mind: This is the training phase, you and your dog will be playing with this item, and it will be in your dog's mouth a lot.

It is a good idea to start with keys because they are easy to wash. Using a leather strap as a key chain might make it easier for your dog to pick up. Toss your keys around and see if your dog will pick up and carry them with the command, "Go find my keys." If she does not, refer to the retrieving section (*See* Page 32).

Toss your keys around and see if your dog will pick them up on command.

Step 2. After playing a retrieving game with your keys, play a game of "find" with them. While your dog is watching, toss your keys into a pile of pillows on the floor. Tell your dog, "Go find my keys." Help your dog look through the pillows if she looks confused. Really praise your dog for finding them even if you helped. Remember to treat your dog with a piece of favorite food and release her with an "OK" after you have taken the keys from your dog's mouth. Keep practicing this game of find in different locations in piles of different things.

- Locate a pile of miscellaneous stuff.

- Sit your dog nearby and let her watch you toss the keys into the pile.

- Send your dog with the command, "Go find my keys."

- Help if necessary.

- Call your dog back with the keys in her mouth.

- Praise, Release, Reward.

Step 3. Repeat Step 2, BUT don't have your dog watch you toss the keys into the pile. This is the "Secret Game of Find."

- Locate a pile of miscellaneous stuff.

- Sit your dog facing away as you toss the keys into the pile.

- Send your dog looking with the command, "Go find my keys."

- Help if necessary.

- Call, your dog back with the keys in her mouth.

- Praise, Release, Reward.

Step 4. Repeat Step 3, except come upon a pile of stuff where you planted your keys earlier and ask your dog to, "Go find my keys." This is the "Surprise Game of Find."

- Plant your keys ahead of time in a pile of miscellaneous stuff.

- Approach the pile with your dog.

- Ask your dog to look for the article with the command, "Go find my keys."

- 🐾 Help if necessary.

- 🐾 Call your dog back with the keys in her mouth.

- 🐾 Praise, Release, Reward.

Step 5. Repeat Step 4, but this time even you don't know where your keys are. This is called, "Help, Your Owner is a Scatterbrain," or "Lose your keys."

- 🐾 Lose your keys.

- 🐾 Come upon your dog.

- 🐾 Ask your dog to look with the command, "Go find my keys."

- 🐾 Help if necessary especially if you are running late.

- 🐾 Call your dog back with the keys in her mouth.

- 🐾 Praise, Release, Reward, and GO to Work!

Step 6. This trick can be done with any typically lost items. Practice by naming the items and teaching your dog these names. Start with something like your keys and the remote.

Play games of fetch with each item *saying the name of the item in the game.* Then place both items out in front of your dog on a piece of rug or peg board. Tie one of them to the rug or peg board with a string. Ask your dog to find the item that is not tied down. If your dog tries to get the wrong item, she won't be able to pick it up. You will *not* need to tell your dog "No" because she isn't doing anything wrong. She is getting something for you and is trying hard, so don't scold.

Just go up to your dog and point to the right item and praise when she picks it up. Try again until the right one is found consistently. Trade off and on with each item by tying and untying. Add different items after you have named them for your dog by playing fetch with them. Then add them to the tie down game. Do steps two through five with each different item. Your dog will earn her keep from now on. The more you practice the more your dog will know.

- 🐾 Play fetch with the command, "Go find—whatever."

- 🐾 Start with two different items over the course of several sessions.

- Tie one item to a rug or peg board.

- Command your dog, "Go find whatever" for the untied item.

- Help if necessary, never reprimand for trying to take the wrong thing. Go and point to the right item.

- Alternate the items.

- Add more items that you have named for your dog.

- Do Steps 2–5 with each item.

"Secret game of Find." You can help if necessary.

Tie different items to a peg board and ask your dog to "Find" the item that isn't tied down.

Step 7. Have friends over and have all of the potentially lost items in a box. Ask someone to hide an item while your dog is out of the room. Then bring your dog in and have her find it.

Don't allow your friends to be too creative in their hiding places. Remember, your dog is your best friend and she doesn't want to make YOU look foolish.

Paper Route

So many times you hear people complain about what their dogs cost them. With dog food, veterinary visits, grooming fees, toys, and who knows what else, the cost is high. The best suggestion you can make to these people, *in good humor,* is to find their dog a part-time job to help with expenses.

Find your dog a part time job.

A good suggestion is a paper route. The first house on the route should be the one where the dog lives. The paper should be delivered from the front porch or yard to the door step. A famous quote worthy of repeating here is, "Every journey begins with just one step." Updated it can be, "Every paper route begins with just one house." *Paper Delivery is truly a trick of Prey Drive.* Your dog doesn't need to have much Prey, but a score better than 30 will make it a lot easier to teach. *Coming back with the newspaper is part of Pack Drive, as any dog coming to you is exhibiting Pack behaviors.*

Step 1. Teach the retrieve using any object, a stick or a ball, it doesn't matter. *See* "Take Me Out to the Ball Game: The Retrieve" (Page 32). The command for the trick is "Take the paper."

Step 2. Teach your dog to hold and carry the newspaper, however it is delivered in your area. *See* "Take Me Out to the Ball Game."

Step 3. Put your dog on leash. It isn't safe for your dog to be out without a leash on. Toss a paper near the delivery spot at your home. Tell your dog to "Take the paper." While your dog is going to get the paper, back up to the front door of your home. When your dog has the paper, call your dog to come to you. When he gets there, take the paper with the command, "Give." Praise with much enthusiasm and release by saying, "OK." Remember to pay your paper boy for a job well done. (I think the going rate for paper delivery is a dog cookie a day.)

- 🐾 Toss the paper.
- 🐾 Send your dog with the command "Take the paper."
- 🐾 Back up to the door, and call your dog to you.
- 🐾 Say, "Give."
- 🐾 Praise and Reward.

Step 4. Pre-plant the newspaper, or right after it is delivered, send your dog for the paper with the command, "Take the paper." Once your dog has the paper, call from the doorway and praise. Say, "Give." Remember to give a reward.

If your dog needs help, go to the paper and point to it. *Don't repeat the command.* If he needs more help, take your dog to the paper and gently put it in his mouth. You are trying to make this fun, not scary. *You are not trying to put your dog into Defense/Flight Drive. Be careful.* If you help your dog by taking the collar, remain friendly and smiling. Watch that you don't tower over your dog with your body posture. *Really praise* whether you helped or your dog did it all alone.

- 🐾 Have the paper outside, don't let your dog see you put it out.
- 🐾 Send your dog with the command, "Take the paper."

- 🐾 Help if necessary.
- 🐾 Call from the doorway with the word "Come."
- 🐾 Praise your dog for coming then say, "Give."
- 🐾 Praise again and release.
- 🐾 Pay your delivery dog the going wage.

Practice makes perfect, and if that dog is ever going to make a living at this, you will need to practice. Have fun!

Tug of War

Tricks can do more than entertain, they can also provide exercise and the release of pent-up energy.

If you have a dog with lots of Prey Drive, what do you do with that dog? To live peacefully with that dog, you need to use up all of that Prey Drive or your dog will be walking on the ceiling. *Therefore, you play lots of ball games and do lots of retrieving to satisfy that Drive.*

To live with a Prey Drive intense dog, you need to play lots of ball to survive.

If you have a dog with lots of Pack Drive, what do you do with that dog? Most likely that dog follows you around the house all the time. *You pet and love on Pack Drive dogs just because they need and thrive on your attention.* If you didn't spend lots of time and have lots of "Face Time" (hugs and kisses) with a high Pack Drive animal, your dog would not thrive and could become nervous or neurotic, causing destructive or barking behavior.

So what do you do with a dog with lots of Fight Drive? Most of the time people try to squelch Fight Drive. They try to "keep a lid on it."

As you can see from the above examples, if you do not give your dog adequate time in the appropriate Drives, problems arise.

A dog with lots of Fight Drive and no outlet, might become a real problem. Fight Drive needs a place to go.

A good outlet for Fight Drive is controlled Tug of War games. Controlled means YOU make up the rules. Any dog can play tug of war, but it can be particularly necessary for some dogs with high Fight Drive.

Before starting any Tug of War games, if your dog has any Fight Drive at all, make sure you have first done the Long Down and Long Sit exercises to establish the correct relationship (*See* Pages 28 and 31). You want the relationship between you and your dog to be understood. Then play and have fun.

Give your dog an outlet for Fight Drive.

Step 1. Get a Tug of War toy. This is something that can be easily grasped by both you and your dog. Cloth and cloth toys work very well. You can actually purchase toys designed for tug. Toss the toy several times for your dog and make sure your dog is interested in it.

Step 2. Offer the tug toy to your dog and keep hold of one end. If he won't take one end from you, then toss it and you take one end from him. Use a phrase to signal your dog to pull, something like, "Who's toy is this anyway?" or "Growl." Growling with your dog will entice most dogs to play tug.

Step 3.   It is okay for your dog to get or win the toy. After all, that is what Tug of War is all about.

But, you need to be able to make your dog "Give" it to you if and when you give the command to do so. Teach the "Give" command. (*See* "Take Me Out to the Ball Game: The Retrieve" Page 32.) If your dog will not give back something, gently twist the toy with one hand and push in slightly on your dog's lips from both sides of the muzzle with the other hand over his nose as you firmly remove the toy from your dog's mouth. Toss it again so your dog doesn't resent your taking it away. It is all right to do this on leash the first few times so your dog doesn't leave with the toy.

Write a tug skit, "This is my paper." "No, it's mine!"

Step 4.   Controlled Tug of War is when *you start* the game and *you finish* it. Your dog should not go away with the toy unless you say, "OK."

A really good game of Tug of War is one when both you and your dog have been successful at winning a few times and the toy has been chased and brought back and played with again and again. Controlled Tug of War has several "Give" commands among the tugs. Play for fun and allow your dog to use up some of that Fight

Drive. This is great exercise, which should not be overlooked. It may be a natural instinct and need for your dog, so fulfill it.

Tug of War can also be considered a Prey Drive game instead of a Fight Drive exercise. In *Fight Drive*, Tug of War is *Me against You*, each of you trying to get the toy. In *Prey Drive*, Tug of War is *Me and You against the Tug Toy*, both parties together trying to kill the toy. *Know your dog's drive numbers to see which way your dog is playing Tug of War.*

Step 5. As a trick, Tug of War can be part of a skit performed for others. The skit is played out as you write it. For example, the tug toy might be a rubber, rolled-up newspaper and your dog is small or a Toy breed. Start the skit with you and your dog fighting over the newspaper. The dialogue can be something like, "Get your own paper next time, this one is mine." Whatever you think of, play it up dramatically about how each of you want this one thing. Occasionally, each of you will get the item. Then, great victory or great disappointment will win the Best Acting Award.

Have fun with this and let your imagination be your limitation.

Read on, there's more!

Let your imagination be your limitation.

Chapter FOUR

Cute Tricks

B eing practical is one thing, but being cute and adorable is what it's all about. What is cuter than playing dress up with a model that has a tail wagging under the clothes? Giving an interview to the best dressed dog in town is always newsworthy. Watching your dog rolling over or giving you "five" may not serve any useful purpose, but wow, what fun. Here is where to start. Expect to keep some giggles in your voice and keep your camera handy.

Let's Play Dress Up

What child doesn't love to play dress up? Well, your dog is no different. Well actually he is, but why not teach your dog to wear things? What is cuter than going to the beach with a sun visor on your dog's head, or going to the parade with sun glasses in the summer?

Some dogs actually want the sweater or rain coat in bad weather, and if you have a dog that requires lots of brushing, you will want it too. When you are putting a dog act together, most tricks will seem even more professional if your dog is dressed for the occasion. Plus, on Halloween think of all the extra treats you will get if your dog goes along with a sack of his own. A crown, an evening dress, a clown suit—the options are limitless. Remember, let your imagination be your only limitation. *Pack Drive will be of great help with this effort. Dogs with lots of Pack Drive enjoy being touched and pampered, and being brushed and getting groomed is something that they enjoy or tolerate without much problem. Wearing clothes is in that same category.*

Step 1. Your dog should be used to wearing a collar. Get a nice buckle collar and then put it on your dog. If the dog scratches at it, try a distraction, and before you know it, your dog will not mind the collar.

Take a bandanna or a large handkerchief, fold it in half diagonally, and tie it around your dog's neck. Your dog will look *very* cool. If your dog accepts this for the day, you are halfway there.

This trick or treat "Easter Bunny" wins the prize.

If your dog tries to scratch it off, just say, "Stop it," and touch the dog to focus attention on you. Smile and pet the dog or throw a ball. Change the focus of your dog's attention.

Step 2. Take another bandanna and tie it around your dog's head and knot it loosely under the chin like a scarf. Smile and give lots of praise. Remember to firmly yet kindly say, "Stop it" if the dog tries to rub it off. Change the subject with a cookie treat or another petting session.

Step 3. Get an old pair of sunglasses, or a child's pair from the dime store. Getting the glasses to stay on your dog's head is the challenge. Tie a string to each ear piece and then tie the two strings together leaving enough room to rest the ear pieces on the dog's ears. The strings will be tied together behind your dog's head, allowing the glasses to rest on top. Now put the bandanna back on your dog's head over the glasses, holding them into place. You now have the cutest grandma in town.

Step 4. Take an old T-shirt or a child's T-shirt (baby size for Toy breeds) and slip it over your dog's head, putting the dog's front legs through the shirt sleeves. It may be necessary to put a small knot in the shirt at the belly so your dog's back legs don't walk on the shirt. Offer a treat and make your dog walk to you with the shirt on. Give lots of praise and make a really big deal about how cute this is. Dogs can be vain. Make sure you give lots of admiration.

Step 5. Putting socks or shoes on your dog can be a little more tricky. They must fit well, as your dog may try to shake them off, but you do not want to tie anything

Dogs will high-step when wearing boots.

Are you prepared to live with a fashion plate?

onto the feet or legs because you might tie it too tight and cut off the dog's circulation.

If you have access to baby socks or slippers, use them as they work quite well—even for the big dogs. If you have an old pair of knit gloves that you don't mind cutting the fingers out of, you can use these to get a dog used to wearing socks. Be prepared for a lot of laughter, as most dogs will walk like a high stepping horse, thinking that they can step out of the socks. Be gentle, and make your dog walk to you for a cookie or another big treat. Most pet stores sell dog boots. These are perfect and can be fitted to your dog.

Step 6. Most pet stores carry clothing items made specifically for dogs. A lot of pattern companies have designs for dogs also, so if you like to sew you will have the best-dressed dog in town. Once your dog can wear and keep the bare essentials on—socks, T-shirts, and bandanas—the rest is up to you.

Have fun and remember to keep your dog's attention on you and not on the clothes. Use food or toys with commands to Come or to Stay. Remember, nothing embarrassing, but make your dog happy and pleased to be a fashion plate. *Lots of praise and treats work as distractions for your dog.* Check with your local humane society for any pet celebration days that might have contests for the best-dressed canine. You are bound to get first prize.

Move the Nose and the Body Follows

One of the simplest things you can do with your dog is to teach following something closely with her nose, for example, a small great smelling piece of food in your hand. I recommend something like beef jerky treats. You can also use small pieces of cut-up cheese or anything else your dog likes. The important thing here is that the dog must be willing to follow your hand with the goodie in it, so make it smell interesting. You move the goodie hand, the nose follows the hand, and the dog's body follows the nose. You can't miss. *Dogs with medium to high Prey Drive find these tricks very easy.*

The Interviewer

You can now ask your dog the questions that you have always wanted to know the answers to and were afraid to ask.

Step 1. Move the hand and you move the nose. Put a small piece of your goodie in your hand and show it to your dog and let her sniff it. Move your hand slowly left and right directly in front of your dog's nose. Watch her follow your hand in a head shaking motion. Let her have a small piece and try it again.

Step 2. Move the goodie slowly side to side for NO and up and down for YES. Treat occasionally for each response. You can add the commands "No" and "Yes" as if you were confirming the answer you received. "No? You didn't chase the neighbor's cat today, No?" or "Yes? You do want another cookie, Yes?"

Step 3. To perfect this trick you must be strong willed. You will want to eliminate your hand as the cue, and replace it with you head.

Kneel in front of your dog and move your goodie hand simultaneously with your head nod or shake. Place the treat in between your lips or teeth and continue to slowly move your head as your dog watches: back

Interview your famous trick dog.

and forth for no and up and down for yes. Give your dog the treat directly by hand. Do not spit it, because that will only teach your dog to stop and stare at your face, carefully waiting for flying treats.

Sit

It is important to be able to have your dog sit on command, and most tricks will require it in one step or another. Sit is one of the most important positions. Dogs with some Pack Drive enjoy the training and the time that you spend with them. They should do well with this as a trick. *Prey Drive is all about food so these tricks are easy for dogs with a reasonable amount of this Drive.*

Step 1. Slowly move your treat hand, keeping your connection with your dog's nose, up and over her head.

Step 2. Say, "Sit" clearly in a commanding voice as you move the food in about a 45 degree angle over your dog's head. Say it only once, and move SLOWLY to keep the food connection with the dog's nose.

Step 3. When your dog is in the Sit position, praise with a goodie.

Step 4. Release with OK, or go right on to the next command, Down.

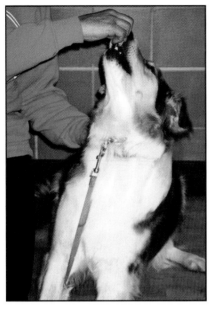

Move your treat hand slowly towards the ground.

Keep your treat hand connected with the dog's nose.

Down

The Down position is extremely valuable when you are establishing the relationship that you will have with your dog. (*See* "The Long Down" Page 28.) *The Down position is good to be in when you share time with a Pack Drive dog. You will also be using food in this trick, so your Prey Drive dog will love it too.*

Step 1. First Sit your dog, either with a treat and command or with only a command. (*See* above.)

Step 2. Say "Down" as you do the following: Show another small treat and SLOWLY move the goodie hand down toward the ground directly in front of your dog's feet. Round your hand slowly when you get close to the ground, bringing the goodie hand out a few inches in front of your dog's feet. Make it like a rounded L-shape, moving very slowly and *keeping the connection with your dog's nose.*

Step 3. Praise and feed the goodie.

Step 4. You can release or move on to the next trick, Roll Over.

Roll Over

Rolling over is when your dog lays on the floor and rolls completely over sideways. This is a crowd favorite and gets lots of applause. *Because of the movement involved with this trick, Prey Drive dogs do very well.*

Step 1. Place your dog into a Down position either with a command only or with a command and a goodie. (*See* above.)

Step 2. Show the goodie hand, and slowly making a small circle around and over your dog's head, say, "Roll Over." Circle over and around your dog's head with the goodie. Try to get your dog to look around over her shoulder while laying on the ground by moving the goodie up and over and around.

Step 3. With your other hand you can pat the floor beside your dog, and then gently help her roll over in that direction. Try again. Circle around with the goodie, pat the floor and gently help her roll over if necessary.

Circle the treat and hand over and around your dog's head and shoulder.

Step 4. Make a really big deal about the roll even if you did all the work. You want your dog to know that the tumble was what you wanted to happen. The only way your dog will get that message is from you. Get your dog really excited about the roll and try again. *If your dog likes being in Prey Drive, use a high pitched voice for enthusiasm.*

Remember, a dog who is high in Defense Flight might get stuck in the upside down position. Be very encouraging and keep your tone of voice very quiet. Watch that you aren't towering over your dog when working this trick. Keep your body upright while you kneel in front of your dog on the floor.

Sit Pretty

This trick makes even the most mischievous dog look sweet and innocent. This trick will soften any heart. Sitting Pretty is when your dog sits up in a begging position and looks at you with those pleading eyes. Pack Drive and Prey Drive are very beneficial for this trick; Pack Drive for the cooperation from your dog, and Prey Drive for the desire for the treat.

Step 1. Sit your dog as above. At a 45 degree angle, lift a goodie over and above your dog's head, saying, "Sit." Remember to move slowly to keep the connection with your dog's nose. Don't feed your dog or give the treat to your dog yet.

Step 2. Instead of giving the treat, SLOWLY move the treat an inch at a time straight towards the ceiling. Move *only* an inch at time, trying to get your dog to sit up in a begging position.

Who can resist such a face?

Step 3. Say, "Sit Pretty" and keep the connection with your dog's nose. Lift an inch, connect and lift an inch. Don't go up too high above the dog's nose or your dog will jump for it. You want your dog to *sit* up, not stand up.

Step 4. After your dog is Sitting Pretty, if your dog knows the word "Stay," you can add it here to help keep your dog balanced on its haunches. (*See* "Stay" Page 21.)

Keep the treat connected with your dog's nose and lift slowly to get your dog to Sit Pretty.

Random Rewards

As you teach your dog to follow your goodie hand, give the treat only *occasionally*. Your dog may be getting quite good, even in one training session, but still only randomly reward with the treat. Make the dog work harder and harder for each treat. Don't stop the treats totally, but rather make each one a true surprise and special treat. Eventually, the treat can come at the end of a whole routine during which your dog has only followed your hand and listened to the commands.

Sneeze, "God Bless You."

Did you know that your dog lets you know when he thinks something is funny? A dog will sneeze. In a way, it is like a little giggle.

Most likely when your dog meets you at the door in the evening, there will be a sneeze along with your greeting. When you start to play on the floor or start to interact directly with the dog you will get a sneeze for your effort. Tell your dog a joke, or trip over something, in general make a fool of yourself and your dog will sneeze (giggle) at you.

One of the best tricks, one that will impress even the un-impressable, is to get your dog to sneeze on command. You will have to learn a lot of new dog jokes for your dog, but it will be worth it. *Pack Drive is necessary for this trick. It is the Pack Drive that makes your dog see the humor in you.*

Step 1. Find out what makes your dog laugh. Most dogs will automatically sneeze at you when you start trying to get them to do something after a period of not paying any attention to them.

Get some food and get your dog. Kneel down with your dog in front of you and say, "Sneeze," and then you sneeze *at your dog.*

Stay totally still with the treat clutched to your chest. Wait. Pretend sneeze again and wait. Wait. If you are starting to look pretty silly, good work, keep it up.

When you get *any* amount of air blown out of your dog's nose, a full sneeze or a partial sneeze, go crazy with praise and give the treat. Do it all again. Remember that to get a full blown sneeze you must reward any attempt to sneeze at all. You are looking silly to your dog, and your dog doesn't realize that you actually want him to laugh at you. You need to make it clear to your dog that you really have gone over the edge.

"You are so funny."

- 🐾 Kneel in front of your dog.

- 🐾 Hold food in your hand to your chest. Do not offer it.

- 🐾 Give the command, "Sneeze" and pretend to sneeze at your dog.

"Yippee, trick training is fun!"

- 🐾 Wait, wait, wait.

- 🐾 Pretend to sneeze again.

- 🐾 When air comes out of your dog's nose,

- 🐾 Give a treat and tons of praise.

Step 2. Practice step one over and over again. Stop and then come back to it. You shouldn't have too much trouble making your dog laugh. Your command is, "Sneeze," but most dogs will sneeze *with* you so practice sneezing with your dog.

Timing is really important with this trick. Your dog must learn that it is the sneezing act that you are rewarding. To accomplish this, you must

Give tons of silly praise.

praise the *instant* you get any air blown out of your dog's nose. This is a fun trick to teach because you end up laughing at each other.

Step 3. When a dog sees the treat but cannot get it, the dog gets excited, which aids in your attempt to get a good sneeze. Once your dog has made the connection to give a full sneeze on the command, "Sneeze" (which is followed by your pretend sneeze), you must always reinforce with food and rewards for even the slightest resemblence of a sneeze from your dog.

Humor makes a team. Learn to laugh at each other.

If you do not, the sneezing will stop. This is very important. Be prepared to reward even the little blows in front of your friends. This will make the next sneeze bigger, not smaller.

Good luck and practice. It never hurts to try this one during allergy season!

Hide and Seek *or* The Great Safari Hunter

This is more a game that you can play with your dog than a trick. You can spend hours playing with your dog in the house on a rainy afternoon— and you should. It is exactly what your dog needs for the good companionship all dogs must have. But, did you know it is exactly what you need as well? It is a proven fact that having dogs makes you live longer. After all, who loves to spend time with you more than your dog?

Obviously Pack Drive is central to Hide and Seek. You can make this a Prey Drive game also, for the thrill of the hunt. You need to be particularly aware of your dog's Flight Drive because a dog can get very scared upon discovering you if you are not careful. With a lot of Prey Drive you may need to add some motivation to the game, but we will cover that.

Who is looking for whom?

When your dog sees you, make sure she comes all the way around the furniture *to* you.

Step 1. You must be able to get away from your dog so that you can hide. *With high Pack Drive dogs this can be tricky because they stick to you like glue.* If necessary, toss a five second treat into another room and walk briskly to an easy hiding place, like behind an easy chair that leaves you mostly exposed. A five second treat is something that your dog will not swallow whole, yet also won't lie down to eat and then stay there. A small dog cookie works well.

Step 2. Wait a few seconds to see if your dog comes looking for you. *Dogs really high in Pack Drive will look for you automatically when they realize you are not in sight.* If you can peek around a crack in the chair, it is fun to watch your dog looking for you. If your dog is not in sight, make a noise: *a whistle or squeak for Prey Drive, or your dog's name for Pack Drive stimulus.* Stay slightly hidden.

Step 3. Make sure your dog comes all the way around the furniture *to* you when she sees you. Give a treat reward or a big hug, *depending on your dog's Drives. Finding you at all will make your dog's Pack Drive come alive, while a cookie treat for finding you will make the Prey Drive in your dog happy.*

Here is where you need to be careful. You want your dog to *enjoy* finding you. That is the game: looking for you, then finding you.

If you scare your dog when he finds you, even accidentally, you will not encourage your dog to ever look for you again. Instead, your dog may become nervous when he doesn't see you in fear that you may pop out of no where. *Dogs with much Flight Drive and/or little Fight Drive can become stressed unless you let them find you quietly with a smile on your face.* Say nothing and let them adjust to you. Dogs with high Flight Drive will love this unless you become a jack-in-the-box from behind the door.

Step 4. Gradually make your hiding places more difficult. Start out in the open, then go under the tables, then behind doors left ajar, and finally to really challenging places like in closets with the door left open only a few inches. Let your imagination be your limitation.

- Distract your dog in another room.

- Hide.

- Make a noise or call your dog.

- Be quiet and let your dog hunt for you.

- Wait to be found, and reward your dog for a job well done.

Give Me a Kiss

As a dog lover, you will want to show affection to your dog. What is more rewarding than the unconditional love your dog returns?

Having a pet can add years to your life with the pet's love reducing the stress that builds up, or so the scientific world has said. Now it is time to give some of that love back in return. Pack Drive is an absolute necessity for this trick. A dog with no Pack Drive at all will not want to kiss you no matter what you do. It would be like kissing your little brother or sister—*no way!* So to make sure you are not wasting your time, check your dog's score and make sure there is some Pack Drive, the more the better.

Step 1. If your dog is large, sit your dog on the floor and kneel next to him. If your dog is small, pick him up in your arms. Either way, make sure your dog is in Pack Drive by petting and smiling at your dog. Be very careful about your body posture by not standing and bending over, but rather by kneeling or sitting next to your dog if he is on the floor. *You need to have your dog attentive to you and in Pack Drive for this trick.*

Step 2. After giving your dog a hug, say, "Give me a Kiss." Make a kiss-kiss sound (smacking your lips) and present your kisser to your dog. If you get no response, make the kiss-kiss sound again. *Don't repeat your "Give me a Kiss" command; rather, gently blow into your dog's face and make the kiss-kiss sound. If your dog's highest Drive is Defense/Fight, do not attempt to blow in his face unless you have done the Long Down, Long Sit, section in this book successfully (See Pages 28 and 31).*

If your dog gives you a kiss (licks your face), give lots of praise and let your dog lick you as long as you wish. Make sure you show praising acceptance of the kiss and do not act upset about your wet face. This will only serve to discourage your affectionate pooch.

Step 3. Repeat Step 2 often at different times during the day. Make your dog understands the "Kiss" command so that you can ask for a kiss anytime, and get one. After all, isn't that a fantasy come true? Ask for a kiss and get a kiss. Okay, okay, it's from a dog, but a rose by any other name would smell as sweet, and a kiss is a kiss. Remember to release your dog and give lots of hugs in return for the kiss.

Problem Solving: If you are unsuccessful in getting your dog to kiss you by putting him into Pack Drive, and if a gentle blow of air doesn't work

What is more rewarding than the unconditional love you get from your dog?

either, then it is time to resort to temptation. Very few dogs need this solution, but just in case, here it is. Follow step one but instead of Step 2, lightly put something tasty at the spot you want your dog to lick (kiss). For example, a touch of butter, peanut butter, or cheese rubbed on the spot will do the trick.

Give the "Give me a Kiss" command and present your tempting, smelly face. After a short sniff you are bound to get a lick. Remember to praise for the kiss. Repeat until you can use less and less of a tempting dab. Always give a clear command so that you are teaching the command. Praise your dog appropriately and then release with lots of hugs.

Step 4. Use your "Give me a Kiss" command between other tricks as part of your act. It serves as both a great crowd pleaser and your dog will start to view it as a break because of the interaction between you. Getting a kiss and giving a kiss can be a lot of fun, but then you probably already knew that.

Easter Egg Hunt

Once a year you can have your dog join in on the Easter Egg Hunt or every night you can play find the cookie and challenge your dog's nose to find the hidden dog treat. After all, you are not a gum ball machine that just hands out goodies, and your dog should work at finding that rawhide chew or toy. *Prey Drive is a must for this trick. You are teaching your dog to hunt out food. That is exactly what Prey Drive is all about, rummaging and obtaining food.*

Step 1. Start out with a dry treat that has a good odor, like a slice of dog beef jerky. Put a pile of old newspapers on the floor and spread them out a little. Call your dog to you and show him the slice of jerky. Tell your dog to Stay (*See* Page 21) and hide the slice between several bundles of paper. Tell your dog it is now time for the hunt to begin. Release your dog from the Stay with an "OK" (release word) and give the "Hunt" or "Find it" command. Encourage your dog to continue looking as your dog's nose begins to investigate the pile. If interest begins to lessen or if your dog is not having a quick success finding the treat, start lifting a layer of the paper to reveal an edge of the prize. *Make a big deal about your dog's success.*

If the find was easy, do it again. If the find was a little difficult, make it a little easier this time and don't put the treat or prize too deep into the pile of papers. By using a high pitched voice and encouraging words like "hurry," "find it," "you can do it," and "hurry up," you will be keeping your dog in Prey Drive. Since this is needed to hunt for and find food, it will increase your dog's success at finding the "Easter Egg." So keep it up and remember to use a high-pitched voice to elicit the Prey Drive.

Step 2. After hunting through the pile of papers has been successful, try hiding the food elsewhere in the room. Some examples would be in the couch pillows, among the shoes on the floor, and under the throw rug at the door.

Sherlock Dog

This trick is similar to the hot/cold game you may have played as a child. You may remember that if you were close to the item, you were told you were getting hotter, or colder if you were moving away from the item.

Sherlock Dog can sniff out anything.

You are your dog's coach. Help by pointing and guiding. If your dog is getting colder, use your voice for encouragement. Make if fun for your dog by planning frequent successes.

A word of caution: *Do not hide food on the coffee table.* One of the house rules should be that food on the coffee table belongs to the *people* in the house—never to the dog. You should teach your dog this rule. Do not sabotage yourself by putting accessible food on the coffee table and encouraging your dog to take it.

You should spend some time teaching—*No stealing food from the coffee table.* You can easily do it by simply setting the situation up with your dog. Put a piece of pizza or cheese on the table and have your dog walk by on leash, if he does more than a casual sniff, check your dog with the leash and collar and keep walking. Continue this and sit next to your dog while *you* are eating at the coffee table, but never let your dog have food *there.* If you are consistent and patient, you can teach your dog anything you want to.

Step 3. Impress your houseguests with your Sherlock Holmes Dog who can sniff out anything. Plant an edible dog prize somewhere in the room and call your dog to find it for your friends. This can be great fun for all. Remember to use your Prey Drive voice to aid your Sherlock as Dr. Watson would help when necessary.

Step 4. At Easter time, boil some eggs and peel them. Hide them during the Easter Egg Hunt for your dog to find. This way it truly becomes a family affair. *Don't let your dog find too many*. We all can eat too much at holidays if we are not careful, so can your dog.

Get In, Go Through

Now that you can *stop* your dog from crossing a threshold (*See* "Door Manners" Page 39), the opposite can be just as rewarding. Teach your dog to *go through* an opening. This can be handy for getting your dog in a crate for housebreaking, problem chewing, in hotels when traveling, or at the veterinarian or groomer. You can use it for many tricks too, like getting the dog to hide under the table or in the tricks below.

Teaching the command, "Get in" is very easy. If you have a crate you can use it, or get a cardboard box and lay it on its side. You can also use your closet as long as the floor has plenty of space. You will need some food and a hungry dog. *The higher your dog's Prey Drive, the more your dog will like food training.* Pack Drive dogs may not want to leave you, so make sure you use food they really like to entice them to leave you for the food.

"Get In" or "Go Through."

Step 1. Get your box, your food, and call your dog to join you. Show your hungry dog a small piece of food and toss it into the box. Make sure it is not a scary looking box, *especially if your dog has much Flight Drive.* Say, "Get in," and toss the food into the box, crate, or closet. Do not shut your box as it doesn't matter if your dog comes back out with the treat to eat it. The important thing is that he went in to get the treat on command.

- 🐾 Say, "Get in."

- 🐾 Toss in the treat.

- 🐾 Praise your dog and say what a clever dog she is.

- 🐾 Say, "OK," and allow your dog to come out.

Do this several times over the course of several training sessions until your dog willingly runs in to get the treat.

Step 2. Now you *want* your dog to get in *before* getting the treat. Tell your dog, "Get in," then give the treat after your dog goes into the opening. This will cause your dog to wait for the treat inside. Hand it in *immediately at first*, then gradually make your dog wait a few extra seconds before getting the treat. You can say, "Wait," if your dog is coming back out immediately. (*See* "Door Manners" Page 39.)

- 🐾 Say, "Get in." Allow your dog room enough to go in.

- 🐾 Hand in the treat after your dog crosses into the opening.

- 🐾 Say, "Wait," if necessary.

- 🐾 Praise your dog as he eats the treat.

- 🐾 Say, "OK," and allow your dog to exit the box.

Step 3. You can use this command anytime you want your dog to go through an opening without you going first.

"Wait" before coming out.

After making your dog *wait* at the car door (see Door Manners), say, "*Get in,*" so your dog will jump into the car or onto the wagon tail-gate. It is a very useful command.

Let your imagination be your limitation to where and when you use your "Get in" command. To your dog, "Get in" means the same as "Go Through." Don't forget you can use it that way too, either to allow the dog to go *through* an opening *or into* a small space.

My Dog is a Cat in Disguise!

Cats love to rub themselves on your legs in a figure "8" pattern. This is something that dogs do not typically do on their own, but you can teach your dog to do it. *Dogs with lots of Pack Drive should find this to be fairly easy. A little Prey Drive will help because you can use food to help focus your dog's attention o n your hands.*

    The command for this trick will be, "Be a kitty cat?" Use this before starting each step of the trick.

    You will be using your "Get in" command (*See* Pages 84 and 85) to teach your dog what to do while learning the trick. Remember that "Get in" also means "Go through." To your dog, these two actions are the same. Going into a box or going through the opening results in the same action, therefore you use the same command. You also need to think of it as the same to be consistent.

Doing the figure "8"

Step 1. Get your dog to Sit and Stay near you. (*See* "Sit Stay" in Chapter 2.) Stand with your legs apart and your back to the dog. Have small bits of food in both of your hands.

        Ask your dog, "Be a kitty cat?" Bend forward and show your dog a small piece of food from your right hand between your legs. Say, "Get in" (Go Through). Your dog should come *through your legs* to get the treat. Give the treat and praise your clever dog.

       🐾 Face away from your sitting dog.

       🐾 Tell your dog, "Be a kitty cat?"

       🐾 Stand with your legs apart and show a treat with one hand between your legs.

       🐾 Say, "Get in," and tempt your dog through with a treat.

- Praise your dog for coming through and let him have the treat.

- Repeat until your dog is willingly walking through on command.

Step 2. Start over and have food in both hands. Command your dog to walk through your legs. This time, before giving the treat, guide your dog around your right leg with your right hand until your left hand is visible between your legs. Say, "Get in," again. This time offer the treat with your left hand after the dog has come through your legs the second time. Your dog is now starting to make a figure "8" around your legs.

- Face away from your sitting dog.

- Say, "Be a kitty cat?"

- Open your legs and show a treat with your right hand.

- Say, "Get in," and tempt your dog with a treat guiding around your right leg.

Showing your dog a treat and guide the dog through your legs.

- Show your left hand between your legs with a food treat.

- Say, "Get in," and get your dog to come through again.

- Praise your dog for coming through and let him have the treat from your left hand.

- Repeat until your dog is willingly walking through and around your right leg and through your legs again on command.

Step 3. Continue in the same fashion as in Step 2, except get your dog to go around your left leg too. This will complete the full figure "8" around your legs. Let your dog get the treat after going through your legs three times. The first time to start, the second time after going around your right leg and the third time after going around your left leg.

- Say, "Be a kitty cat?" to start the trick.

- With your dog behind you, command, "Get in" and show right hand with food.

- Guide around your right leg and then show treat in the left hand from between your legs. Say, "Get in."

- Guide around your left leg and show treat in the right hand from between your legs. Say, "Get in."

- Praise and release and give your food treat.

- Repeat until your dog circles both of your legs without any problems.

Guide around both legs, one after the other.

Step 4. Keep your dog going around your legs several times without a release word. You may need to give a few small treats while your dog is walking around your legs. This will ensure following your hands as they guide the dog around your legs. That is why you will need to have several treats in both hands.

Keep practicing until your dog understands going around your legs without getting treats all the time. Remember your command, "Be a kitty cat?" Then help your dog get started and use your hands to guide—more as signals than treat dispensers. Make sure you always end the trick with an "OK" release word and lots of treats and praise. *Have fun.*

Serpentine Walker

Have you ever seen a snake weave in and out of weeds? You can teach your dog to weave in and out of your legs even while you walk!

Your dog can walk through your legs and cross through again when you take your next step. By using your "Get in" command this trick becomes very easy.

This is a Prey and Pack Drive trick because Prey is stimulated by movement (you will be moving and your hands will be swinging during this exercise) and Pack Drive dogs like working with you—and this trick takes real teamwork.

Step 1. Teach your dog to do the "My Dog is a Cat in Disguise" routine as above.

Step 2. Now all you have to do is to start walking as your dog does the figure "8" pattern around your legs. Don't rush the stationary portion of this trick. Take the transition from standing to walking slowly. After one step, praise and release your dog with a treat. Remember to help guide your dog with your hand holding a treat. Get the focus first on your right hand and then on your left, as you guide the dog around your legs.

Step 3. Guide your dog around your right leg. Then, step forward with your left leg and guide the dog around that leg. Step forward with your right leg and guide him around that leg

Now start walking as your dog goes through and around your legs.

as you step forward with your left leg. Release your dog and remember to give a treat and lots of praise.

As your dog becomes confident about moving with you, it will not be necessary to bend over as far because the dog will be better able to focus on your hands between your legs. This will be

Guide your dog around your leg as you step forward and begin to walk.

Gradually speed up so your dog walks around your legs as you walk on.

very helpful for your back! (Depending on the size of your dog, this trick can be a real back breaker for you.) A little dog takes lots of bending, but a larger dog takes just about as much because you will be teaching your dog to duck through your legs. Holding the treats lower as your dog comes through your legs will help teach the dog to lower her head as she comes through.

Step 4. Gradually speed up your steps, but never *too* fast because your dog needs to make it all the way around your legs with each step. The command you give for this trick is up to you. You can still use "Be a kitty cat," but you are walking instead of standing still. Practice makes perfect. So keep practicing.

How Do You Do?

It is customary for people to shake hands when greeting. When you greet a dog, the only difference is that you shake a paw instead. *A dog with much Flight Drive will often offer its paw as a communication of submission. When you see a dog roll over completely when you greet it, it is communicating to you that it knows you are more powerful then it is. The step before rolling over completely can be lifting its paw to you. Therefore, Flight Drive can be helpful when teaching this trick.*

Step 1. Tell your dog to Sit. Praise your dog for doing so, but do not give the release command. If your dog didn't Sit on command, simply tuck the dog's tail into a Sit and *praise anyway.* Offer your right

"How do you do?"

hand palm up, so the dog could lay a paw into your hand. Command kindly to "Shake." If your dog sniffs your hand *ignore it*. Slowly reach between your dog's front legs and lift the right elbow. Slide your hand down to the paw and gently cup it in your hand as you shake it. *Praise tremendously* and then release with an "OK," release word and give either a treat, a big hug, or whatever your dog likes most. Do it over and over until your dog starts to voluntarily lift the leg without any resistance.

- 🐾 Sit your dog.

- 🐾 Offer your open palm and say, "Shake."

- 🐾 Reach in and lift the elbow of the dog's right leg.

- 🐾 Slide up to the paw and gently shake.

- 🐾 Praise lavishly while you are shaking.

- 🐾 Release with "OK."

- 🐾 Reward.

Do Step 1 many times so that your dog has an opportunity to hear the command, "Shake." Dogs learn through and need repetition before being offered the next step.

Step 2. Tell your dog to Sit. Offer your open palm with the command, "Shake." This time *hesitate* before reaching for the elbow. If necessary, after the pause, gently touch the elbow, but then return to the offered palm position.

Give your dog the opportunity to lift a paw. If the dog voluntarily lifts a paw at all, praise exuberantly and take the paw and shake gently. Then release with "OK," and pet your dog or give a treat. Stay at this level until your dog is lifting the paw off of the ground on command. You then take the paw and shake it as any polite person would do.

- 🐾 Sit your dog.

- 🐾 Offer your open palm and say, "Shake."

- 🐾 Hesitate to see if your dog will lift a paw at all.

- 🐾 Reach in and touch the elbow if necessary.

- Return to the "offered palm" position again.

- When the paw is lifted at all, reach and shake it.

- Praise while you are shaking; make sure you have a big smile.

- Release with "OK."

- Reward, yippee.

Step 3. At this step when you offer your open palm with the command, "Shake," your dog should lift the leg, even if only slightly. Reach for the palm and gently shake as you smile and praise. Then release your dog with the "OK" release word and reward.

- Sit your dog.

- Offer your open palm and say, "Shake."

- When your dog lifts his paw, even slightly, take it.

- Shake the paw while you smile and praise.

- Release and Reward.

Hesitate before reaching for the elbow so your dog will start to lift a paw for the handshake.

Give Me Five

As I'm sure you know, "Give me five" is when you offer your open palm and someone else slaps it. This trick will work wonderfully if your dog offers the wrong hand while teaching the "How Do You Do" trick. Whenever you offer your open palm and your dog gives you the wrong paw to shake, just say, "*You are so cool. Give me five.*" *High Flight Drive makes this trick easy also.* (*See* "How Do You Do" Page 91.)

To teach this as another trick completely, (not just as a saving face response), follow the steps above for shaking hands, but reach for the other paw and give another command.

Step 1. Tell your dog to Sit. Praise your dog for doing so, but do not release. If your dog didn't Sit on command, simply tuck your dog's tail into a Sit and praise anyway. Offer your right hand palm up, so your dog can lay a paw into your hand.

Aim for your dog's left foreleg, the opposite one from shaking hands. Command kindly to your dog, "Give me five." If your dog sniffs your hand ignore it. Slowly reach for and lift the elbow of your dog's left foreleg. Slide your hand down and gently cup the paw in your hand

"You are so cool. give me five."

as you let it lay there for a second. Praise tremendously and then release with an "OK," and either give a treat, a big hug, or whatever your dog likes most. Do it over and over again until your dog starts to slightly lift a leg without any resistance.

🐾 Sit your dog.

🐾 Offer your open palm and say, "Give me five."

🐾 Reach in and lift the elbow of the left leg.

- 🐾 Slide up to the paw and gently hold for a second.

- 🐾 Praise and smile.

- 🐾 Release with, "OK."

- 🐾 Reward.

Step 2. Do as in Step 2 of How Do You Do. Sit your dog. Then offer your open palm with the command, "Give me five." This time *hesitate* before reaching for the elbow. If necessary, after the pause, go in and gently touch the elbow, but then return to the offered palm position. Give your dog the opportunity to lift the paw. If you get the dog to voluntarily lift the paw, praise exuberantly. Take the paw and hold gently. Then release with the, "OK" release word, and pet your dog or give a treat. Stay at this level until your dog is lifting the paw off the ground on command.

- 🐾 Sit your dog.

- 🐾 Offer your open palm and say, "Give me five."

- 🐾 Hesitate to see if your dog will lift the paw at all.

- 🐾 Reach in and touch the elbow if necessary.

- 🐾 Return your palm to the offered position again.

- 🐾 When the paw is lifted at all, reach and hold it for a second.

- 🐾 Praise and give your dog a big smile.

- 🐾 Release with, "OK."

- 🐾 Reward, hurrah!

Step 3. At this step, when you offer your open palm with the command, "Give me five" your dog should lift the leg even if only slightly. Reach for the paw and gently hold it as you smile and praise. Then release your dog with, "OK" and reward.

- 🐾 Sit your dog.

- 🐾 Offer your open palm with, "Give me five."

- 🐾 When your dog lifts a paw even slightly, take it.

- 🐾 Hold the paw while you smile and praise.

- 🐾 Release and reward.

Step 4. Now you can stop holding the paw for a second to make it look like your dog slapped *your* open palm. Tell your dog to Sit. Praise for the Sit. With the command, "Give me five," offer your open palm. When your dog lifts the *left paw*, put your open palm underneath it and slide your dog's paw off. This will look more like the Give Me Five action of slapping.

Your dog is a "Cool Cat." It might not be a good idea to let your dog know this by the way. Some dogs might take offense to being called a cat.

Make the Give Me Five look like a slap rather than a shake.

You Have Food on Your Nose.
"I Know, I'm Saving It for Later."

Balancing food on your dog's nose can be a real crowd pleaser. It can be fun especially when your dog will keep the food there until you say "OK" and even better when the dog tosses it in the air and catches it before it touches the ground.

Dogs high in Pack Drive will most likely have no trouble with this. Prey Drive dogs will view it only as an interference between them and the food on the nose. Let's get started.

Step 1. First you need to cup your hand over the top of your dog's nose. Simply Sit and pet your dog for a few seconds, then cup your hand over the muzzle from the top. If your dog accepts this, you will have no trouble with this trick. *A dog high in Defense/Fight*

"Look Mom, No Hands."

Drive will not easily accept this unless the relationship between you is in order. (See "The Long Down" Page 28.) A dog high in Defense/ Flight might crumble and lie down unless you are very careful about your body posture. Don't lean too far forward; rather, kneel in front of your dog and lean back a bit on your heels.

See if you can cup your hand over the top of the dog's nose.

Step 2. First, Sit your dog in front of you while you are kneeling. Watch your body posture, and lean back on your heels slightly. With one hand, gently hold your dog's muzzle with your thumb on the bridge of the dog's nose and your fingers under the jaw. (If your dog is jumpy, put a finger in the collar first. Then pull the collar up and gently hold the muzzle with your thumb on top, fingers under the jaw, holding the collar too.)

With your *other hand* near the nose, show a small treat and try to get your dog to focus on it. Say, "OK," release your dog and give the treat. Repeat until your dog is truly focusing on the treat without any struggle.

Step 3. Still gently holding the dog's muzzle with one hand, bring the treat up with the other hand and slowly lay it on the dog's nose in front of your thumb. Keep the treat hand close to and in front of the nose and say, "Wait." You can even make it a signal by holding up a finger, as in "wait a minute." After two seconds, say, "OK," and let go of your dog completely. The treat will either fall off or get flipped up into the air. Help your dog find it on the floor and make a big deal about it. Let your dog eat it and give lots of praise. What fun!

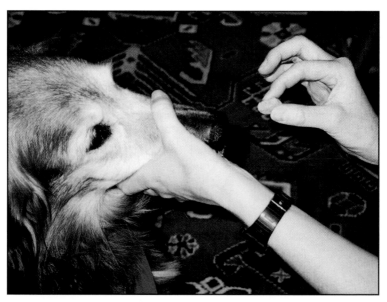

Gently hold you dog's muzzle with one hand and focus your dog's attention on the food in your other hand.

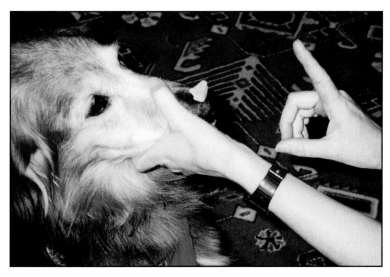

Still holding your dog's muzzle, place the food on the tip of your dog's nose and keep your "Wait" signal in front of your dog's face.

Step 4. As in Step 2, gently hold the muzzle and slowly place the treat on the nose. Add seconds to the "Wait" command and work up to holding the muzzle with your dog balancing the treat for 20 seconds. Keep your finger in front of the dog's face until the time is up. Release and let your dog find the treat.

Slowly let go of the muzzle after placing the food on your dog's nose. Keep your "Wait" signal visible.

By letting your dog find the treat, the dog will flip and catch the treat, or quickly move the muzzle away and catch the treat in mid-air. You might end up with a dog who simply drops it and grabs it. Either way you will end up with a brilliant circus dog.

Step 5. After you set the trick up by gently holding the muzzle and balancing the treat, slowly let go of the muzzle and keep the focus finger in front of your dog's face. Wait just a few seconds, release, and let your dog get the treat. Remember to help your dog find the treat on the floor if necessary.

Step 6. Gradually make the "Wait" time longer and longer. Gradually move the focus finger farther and farther away from your dog's face. If your dog tosses the treat or drops it before the "OK" release word, *you* try to get the treat before the dog, saying, "Try harder." Do it over and shorten either the time or the distance.

Step 7. Show off. Try bigger things, like a big milk bone, or balance a ball. *Let your imagination be your limitation.*

Read on, the best is yet to come!

Chapter FIVE

Hollywood Bound

When people have a talent that is worth noticing, they want to show it off for fame and fortune, of course. Dogs are no different. Skill and excellence are not to be hidden and kept a secret.

Some of the tricks previously mentioned, and all of the tricks that follow, can be worked into an act for your dog that would make talent scouts stand up and take notice. If no one from Hollywood, then possibly someone from the local press or local theaters will notice you. Maybe you'll even get standing ovations from your living room playbill! If that is not enough, then pet therapy groups may be looking for your time and your dog's talents. All you need to do is make your dog a trick-performing dog and advertise that you are available. Have fun and even do some good work at the same time.

"How did you do that?"

The Magic Show is About to Begin!

Magic is always something that sends awe through an audience. Your dog, no matter what age, can achieve magician's status with little effort.

This trick is easy to do in even one training session. It is a rendition of the shell game. The shell game is where someone has three shells and a pea. They put the pea under one shell and then mix the shells up in front of you. You are then to pick the shell that the pea is under. Well your dog, the great magician, will never get it wrong. After one or two tries, your dog will be able to impress audiences far and wide by always being able to find the pea, no matter how many times the "shells" are mixed up and repositioned. *A little Prey Drive will make this trick easy to teach your dog. Pack Drive will be helpful for keeping your dog somewhat balanced when training because you will be using food and this can excite your dog.*

Don't hide talent under a barrel.

Step 1. First you will need three cheap plastic flower pots. (The ones you get when you buy potted plants or seedlings at the nursery.) To make the trick more elaborate, try to find white ones. You can decorate them if you like, but it isn't necessary. If you do, remember that the pots will be upside down for the trick, so decorate accordingly.

The reason the flower pots work better then shells, is that there are holes in the bottom of the pots. Your dog will be using his nose to smell out the food from under the pot. Second you will need dry treats, dog cookies or squares of dog jerky. Cat food works well too because it really smells good to your dog.

Step 2. Place the three pots on the floor and get a pocket of treats. Tell your dog to "Sit and Stay" behind the line of pots. (*See* "Stay" Page 21.) You will kneel down on the other side of the pots.

Show your dog a treat and place it under one of the pots. Tell your dog to, "Find it." Let your dog do whatever it takes to get the treat from under the pot. Usually you will get lots of nudging or pawing at the pot. Once the treat is revealed, let your dog eat it, and praise him for such success. If your dog doesn't stay, you can get another person to hold the dog back until given the command to go. This can add some action to the trick, if you "ham" it up right.

"Which one is it under?"

 🐾 Line up the pots.

 🐾 Place a treat under one, but do not mix up the line.

 🐾 Send your dog to find the right pot with, "Find it."

 🐾 Praise and release your dog.

Step 3. The next step is set up the same with the line of pots between you and your dog. This time, show the treat, place it under one pot, and switch the pots around by one space each. Don't make it too difficult.

- Line up the pots.

- Place a treat under one and move the pot a space or two only.

- Send your dog to find the treat with, "Find it."

- Praise and release your magician.

- Do this step several times, until your dog is getting really good at tipping over or nudging the pot to reveal the treat.

Step 4. Now it is time to test the psychic powers of your magician. Set up for the trick and show your dog the treat. Now mix up the pots as much as you would like. Stop touching the pots. Then command your dog to, "Find it." Yes, your dog is a born entertainer.

- Line up the pots.

- Place a treat under one and move the pots as much as you want.

- Pause after mixing the pots.

- Send your dog to find the treat with, "Find it."

- Praise and release your performer.

- Practice.

The hand is NOT quicker than the nose.

Step 5. Now, to perfect your act for your show, figure out how you are going to "ham it up" about the great "Magician." Things like:

- 🐾 Is the hand quicker then the nose?

- 🐾 This is something not yet seen or done in the canine world.

- 🐾 The one and only, "MY DOG."

Get an audience and try it out. You can even ask an audience participant to guess which one the food is under before sending your magical dog to show everyone which truly is the right one.

Have fun with it. You can even charge admission!

Hula Hoop Jumper

Hula hoops are not just for toning up the waistline. They make a great portable jumping arena for all sorts of entertainment. After your dog can jump through a hula hoop, you can teach your dog to jump through it while anyone holds the hoop. This is usually a great hit with kids and senior citizens. If you use your dog for pet therapy or school visits, you can't miss. If your dog is one that has lots of energy and needs lots of exercise, what better exercise in the winter and during the rainy season than having jumping sessions in the house. *Jumping is part of Prey Drive. Therefore, if your dog has any Prey Drive at all, you can teach it this trick. The more Prey Drive, the easier it will be.*

While on leash, coax the dog through the hula hoop with a treat.

Get a hula hoop that matches your dog's size—they do come in different diameters. If you have a smaller breed, you may want to eventually get several sizes and make it part of the act to keep making the circle smaller and smaller, therefore making the trick tougher and more impressive.

Step 1. Lay the hoop on the ground and take your dog over to see and smell it. Don't force your dog to do anything in particular; just let the hoop be seen on the floor.

Step 2. Put your dog on leash and walk toward the hoop and then over it. If your dog jumps it, that is okay. If your dog walks on it, that is fine, too.

Step 3. Pick up the hoop and rest the bottom edge on the floor while you hold the top.

With your dog still on leash, thread the leash through the hoop and coax your dog through the hoop with the command, "Jump." You can coax with the offer of a treat or by touching the floor and smiling. Once your dog is through the hoop—even walking through it—give lots of praise and a cookie reward. Do this several times until your dog is really going through without much coaxing. Still thread the leash through and have the hoop resting upright on the floor.

Step 4. With your dog on leash, thread the leash through the hoop and raise it off of the floor just a few inches. Say, "Jump," and help your dog hop over the bottom end of the circle, going through the hoop. Remember to give lots and lots of verbal praise and occasionally a food treat as rewards.

Repeat this step until you have the hoop out in front of your dog at eye level. You want your dog to take a few running steps towards the hoop and jump up and through it. Your dog will still be on leash to help guarantee success of the jump and response to the command.

Step 5. Now that your dog understands to go through the hoop, and the command for that action is "Jump," it is time to make it a spectacular trick.

Take the leash off, and present the hoop in front of the dog. Keep it at a level that your dog already does with ease. Say, "Jump" and allow the dog to jump through. Give lots of praise and a food treat. Challenge your dog slightly by holding the hoop at different levels for each jump, sometimes at your dog's knee level, or sometimes at shoulder or eye level. If your dog is of good health and physically fit, it is not unreasonable to present the jump one and one-third times your dog's height at his shoulders. Some breeds can easily jump higher, as much as one and one-half times their height. Know what your dog's capabilities are and be fair. Always make sure that your dog will have firm footing when landing. It is not a good idea to do jumping on vinyl or hardwood flooring or wet grass. Remember that your dog is an athlete and needs to warm up before doing a really high jump.

Step 6. Teach your dog to jump with you pivoting in a circle with the hula hoop moving around you. Make it easy and slow at first, then see how far you can challenge you dog.

Step 7. If you have a really high jumper who takes a broad, stretching jump over the hoop, try to teach the dog to jump the hoop when it is parallel with, but off the ground. First lay the hoop down and teach your dog to jump OVER it on leash. Then hold the hoop up off the ground (horizontal) and ask your dog to jump over it that way. You can really make your act impressive by having your dog sometimes jump *through* the hoop and other times, *over* it horizontally.

Step 8. Add a tutu. (*See* "Dress Up" Page 67.) This can be a real circus act if you use your imagination and add a net skirt to your dog's waist. A crown on the dog's head *and* a tutu can make your ballerina a real crowd pleaser by jumping great heights through the hoop. Everyone will want to try holding the hoop.

Step 9. Have someone else hold the hoop and teach your dog to jump through it on command. If necessary, go back to steps three and four and repeat those steps on leash with your partner holding the hoop as instructed. This is great fun for your friends, so add it to your dog's repertoire.

Work up to step six with your friend's help. There isn't a child alive who will not want to try to get your dog to jump through the hoop once they see you doing it. Another individual holding the hoop changes the trick for your dog, so that part needs to be

Jumping through the hoop can be a real circus act.

taught. Don't expect your dog to do it without practice, *especially if your dog has Flight Drive over 30.* Teach your dog that it is just fine to do the trick while another holds the hoop. Have fun.

Step 10. The most spectacular aspect of this trick is if you can get your dog to jump through the hoop once you have added paper. Tissue paper taped to the hoop will break when you dog jumps through. What a finale.

Start by taping tissue to the hoop with a hole cut in the center for your dog to see through. After the paper is no longer a problem, make the hole in the paper smaller and smaller, until it isn't necessary to have a hole at all. This will be the hit of the act.

Remember the purpose of the paper is to make a spectacular finish, not to scare your dog, so be careful when introducing the paper. If your dog is high in Defense Flight Drive, you might not want to do this step. Know your dog's limitations.

Jump Through My Arms

If a hula hoop isn't handy (or even if it is), why not get your dog to jump through your arms? With only such readily available equipment required, this trick is one that you can always readily show off. The Only Warning Is That Your Dog Should Be of Appropriate Size to Fit through Your Arms.

It would be dangerous to try this with a really large dog if she won't fit through your arms. A friend of mine told her adult Labrador to jump through her arms and ended up with a bruised jaw when the dog obligingly did it and knocked her cold. So use caution.

Jumping is a Prey Drive trick, so a score of over 30 on the test will make this a lot easier. If your dog is high in Defense/Flight, your body posture of bending over and toward your dog may cause some stress, so be particularly careful if your dog has a lot of Flight Drive. After all, you do not want to cause your dog to be fearful. Remember, this should be FUN.

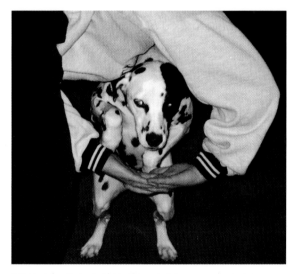

Get your dog to jump through your arms—you always have them with you!

Step 1. First you need to teach your dog the "Jump" command by using the hoop (*See* Page 105). It is much easier to teach the jump command while using some*thing* for your dog to *jump through*, rather than part of yourself. Put your dog on a leash and get a hula hoop. Do steps one through five of the hoop tricks. Step five is where the dog is jumping the hoop off-leash. This is where you need to be *before* you can expect your dog to jump through your arms.

Step 2. As a review progression, practice the jump command several times while going through the hoop. This is necessary to warm your dog up and refresh the command in your dog's mind. Afterwards, put the hoop down and get your dog's attention with a treat. This puts your dog into Prey Drive, which you want for the jump command. The treat doesn't reward your dog before doing something, but rather guarantees that your dog will be ready to jump by eliciting Prey Drive so that the dog will go after the treat.

Squat down and watch your body posture—don't bend over. Instead, squat and make a big vertical circle with your arms out to the side. Give the "Jump" command and encourage your dog. Pause if your dog doesn't respond, instead of repeating your command. Tap your lower arm forming the circle with your upper hand to encourage your dog through. Smile and tilt away from your dog again, trying to elicit Prey Drive even more. When your dog jumps through, remember to give a lot of praise and reward with a treat.

If your dog is hesitant to make the transition from a hoop to your arms, it may be necessary to employ someone to help you. Use a helper's arms as the hoop and put the leash on your dog, threading the leash through your helper's arms. Tap your friend's arms and encourage your dog to jump through.

After a few repetitions, try it again with your own arms. Once you are successful with your own arms, stop after a successful jump. Do something else for a few minutes and then come back to it later. You want your dog to think about the correct response and end on a good note. Keep working at this step until your dog is successful every time you offer your encircled arms to jump through.

Step 3. Next, teach your dog to jump over your extended leg. Kneel on one knee and extend your other leg out to the side.

If you have a small dog, have your leg straight out. If you have a larger dog who is capable of higher jumps, bend your leg at the knee to make a higher jumping obstacle. Give the "Jump" command and tap your leg. Make a sweeping motion with your arm to encourage your dog over. Give lots of praise and reward that jumping dog of yours.

If you need to help your dog, remember to give a treat before you give the command to guarantee your dog is in the right Drive, Prey Drive. Try both the left and the right legs. Have fun with this.

Step 4. Once your dog can jump through your arms and over each leg, there is no end to what you can get your dog to jump over; another dog, an item left on the floor, even your kids will never pose too great an obstacle.

Always remember that you need to review the command and put your dog into Prey Drive first. If you need to, lead your dog to jump the new obstacle with a leash first, in order to do it correctly. Let your imagination be you limitation.

Bobbing for Apples

This trick is just what it implies. You will teach your dog to stick her head into water to retrieve a prize. It might be the already favorite toy or ball, or it might be something new, like a rock or any dropped item, or it can be simply food. This trick is for dogs that are easily motivated to play with something, or those that like to eat. *Most dogs with any Prey Drive at all fall into one of those two categories. Fight Drive will help also because sticking the head into water takes some self confidence, which Fight Drive gives to dogs.*

Things you will need:

You can teach your dog to "bob for apples."

- 🐾 Start teaching this trick with food items that float, like hot dogs, dog or cat food or dog cookies. Work up to things that sink, like some balls, foods, or any thing that your dog can carry that will sink to the bottom.

- 🐾 A heavy bowl that matches the size of your dog. Your dog needs to be able to reach the bottom of the container comfortably. A five gallon bucket will eventually work for a Labrador, but start smaller. A mixing bowl works for Toy breeds. The container needs to be heavy enough so that it won't get pushed along when your dog tries to grab the item.

🐾 A water source or pitchers of water.

🐾 A towel or two (a must). *Maybe* for you and your dog, but *definitely* for the floor.

Let's get started. Start at a time when your dog is hungry, not just after a meal. Since you will be using food initially, your dog will need to be motivated *by the food*. As you know, food is not as motivating after a big meal.

Step 1. Set your container on the floor with towels underneath—no water yet.

Step 2. Drop a piece of food in, and tell your dog to, "Go Bobbing." You can also use a fetch term like, "Go get it," but you are teaching a new trick so you will want to use a new command. Start with "Go get it" if your dog needs help understanding what it is you are trying to communicate. Your dog will learn quickly. Let your dog get the food and give lots of praise for taking it. Then say, "OK" and really make a fuss over your dog.

Step 3. Repeat until your dog is diving into the empty container for the food.

Step 4. Add an inch of water. Do not use very much because you do not want your dog to go under water yet. Drop your food and say, "Go Bobbing." Make a really big deal about your dog's fishing the food out of the inch of water. Your dog has just accomplished a great task. Let your dog know how pleased you are.

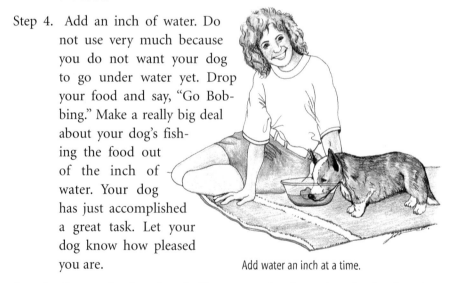

Add water an inch at a time.

Step 5. Stop and take a break. Since your dog is getting the food each time, you want to end when your dog is still wanting more.

Step 6. On the next training session, repeat steps 2 and 4.

Step 7. Add another inch of water. Increase the depth of water slowly. Unless you have a water baby, your dog will need to get used to opening his mouth under water. Floating food will make grabbing it slightly frustrating if the food gets pushed away, so help your dog if necessary. Push the food toward your dog, and hold it steady in the water. Remember to make a really big fuss about any success.

Step 8. Gradually add water to your container until the amount of water is not an issue. *Always end a training session when your dog is still wanting more.* Don't let your dog get tired and bored.

Step 9. Go back to Step 4 (only an inch of water), except use something that will sink. Different types of food will sink or use a ball if your dog really likes to play ball. Continue in the same fashion, going through the steps, gradually adding water.

Remember to keep the size of your dog in mind and keep it fun. *If your dog is high in Flight Drive, do not progress too rapidly or lose your patience.* Teaching something new can be stressful to your dog, and a dog with high Flight Drive can not learn if allowed to stress. Quit and do something fun for your dog.

Step 10. Back up at any point when your dog balks at putting his head under water. You must add the water gradually—very gradually for some dogs. At any point you can start to show off your "Bobbing Trick." Your dog need not completely immerse his head for you to have a real crowd pleaser. *Half of the trick is your showmanship.* Show off your dog with flair.

Dance the Night Away

Fred and Ginger, John Travolta, and Gloria Estefan have nothing on a dancing dog. With just a few simple lessons you can have the dancing partner you have always dreamed about. The dance may not resemble the waltz or the two step, but it will be spectacular in every way. Prey Drive will give your dog the motivation to learn to dance, and Pack Drive will give you a willing partner. Let's have some fun.

Step 1. As you learned in "Move the Nose and the Body Follows" (*See* Page 70), you can manipulate the whole dog by simply controlling the nose. Get a morsel of food and position your dog into a Sit (*See* Page 71) by moving the food close to your dog's nose and then up and backwards *slowly*. Make sure your dog's nose is toward the ceiling and over the head, toward the tail.

Say "Sit." Give your dog the treat. Instead of releasing your dog from the Sit position, connect the scent of another piece of food with your dog's nose and slowly lift the treat straight up above your dog's head.

Command your dog to "Dance." As your dog stands up, lift the food higher and higher until your dog is standing on her hind legs only. Some dogs are better balanced than others, so be patient. Give the treat after just a second of success, so your dog gets the idea and will do it again. Each time try to make the dog stand longer, but increase the time *by seconds only*. Release with "OK" and a treat.

Step 2. Once your dog is standing all the way up on the hind legs and stretching for the food on command, it is time to teach that dog of yours to *really dance*. Remember that before you give the treat, *release* with "OK" and *then feed* your dog. This will teach your dog that the "Dance" command, *rather than the treat*, is the cue word.

Tell your dog to "Dance" and move the food treat in different directions, forward, sideways, backwards, forward again, and so on. Keep your dog up on the hind legs for as long as possible, but keep in consideration your dog's balance and body build. Be fair and patient. Always *release* your dog and *then give* the treat.

Step 3. You can add a second command, "Twirl," to your dancing dog. The Twirl command asks your dog to spin while on the hind legs and to dance in a circle. Simply make small circles with your hand or the food above your dancing dog's head and say, "Twirl." This is quite spectacular once your dog learns what you mean. The only way for that to happen is for this dancing duo to practice.

- First command "Dance." (Raise dog to hind legs.)
- Move dog around for specific amount of time.
- Command "Twirl." (Guide dog around in a circle.)
- Give the Release command and let your dog drop to the floor. Reward.
- Repeat again. Dropping and treating can become part of the dance.

Step 4. Dress for the occasion. A tux or tiara can be very apropos. (*See* "Let's Play Dress Up" Page 67). By adding a dancing wardrobe, your dog can look like a Spanish Dancer, a Ball Room Dancer, a Hip-Hop Dancer, a dancer for the Blues, Rap, you name it. You should dress to look the part also. Let your imagination be your limitation.

Die, You Mongrel, Die

Playing dead is an old favorite from way back. The whole trick consists of aiming your index finger and "firing" at your dog, with the dog falling to the floor pretending to be dead. Playing with guns is never a good idea, but playing with a loaded finger is usually not too dangerous. If your dog doesn't "Die" on the first command, you can always plead that you are a poor aim or that your finger malfunctioned.

Defense/Flight Drive will make this trick easy to teach. Most dogs that have high Flight Drive (30 or higher) are usually willing to lie down and rollover to show their belly. This is the "play dead" position. When your dog rolls over and shows the belly *without* a command, it is usually because you have elicited the Defense Drive either with your body language or your voice so your dog is in Defense/Flight. A dog high in Fight would not naturally exhibit this behavior. So you will have to teach the roll over first.

Step 1. Review the Down command and the Roll Over command from "Move the Nose and the Body Follows" (*See* Page 70).

Step 2. If you have a smaller dog, kneel and bend forward toward your dog. If your dog is larger, bend over at the waist. *Remember you are trying to elicit Defense Drive.* First, give the Down command, but do not release your dog from the Down position. Hide a piece of food in your "gun" hand. With a deep, low, strong tone in your voice, say "Bang."

With your gun hand, point down and directly at your dog from above, as you give the strong "Bang" command. A dog with high Flight Drive will roll upside down. With your gun hand, show and give the treat while the dog is still upside down. Then, with a big happy voice, release your dog with "OK." This should help your dog to get out of the Defense/Flight Drive mode in order to get up and play as a reward.

🐾 Down your dog.

🐾 Hide a piece of food in your "gun" hand.

- Use bent over body posture and a strong deep voice.

- Say "Bang." Make it sound like a gun shot.

- Give the hidden food from your "gun" hand.

- Release with "OK."

- Play with your dog to get back into Pack Drive from Flight.

If your dog does not collapse into Flight Drive, keep the gun finger pointing and show the treat in that hand over your dog's head to get the dog to roll over, but use your other hand to keep the dog from rolling all the way over. Give the treat from your "gun" hand. Try to keep your dog in the "dead" position for a few seconds. Then release with *lots of enthusiasm*.

Step 3. Now you are going to do the same as in step two, except not from a Down position. When your dog is attentive, you can use the dog's name if necessary, your body posture, and a deep tone of voice. Give your dog the "Bang" command to die.

Of course first *load* your "gun" with a treat in your hand. Use the same techniques as in step two to help your dog to get in the roll over position. Some dogs will lie completely on their backs with their feet towards the sky. Others will simply lie on one side. It will depend on the amount of Defense/Fight and Flight as to which "dead" position your dog will use. Don't worry about this point. The "Bang" command makes your dog drop "dead." That is the result of being "shot." After all, dead is dead. You can't be sort of dead. Whether on the side or on the back, your dog is play-acting "dead." So don't forget to say "OK" to bring your dog back to life.

Step 4. Now that your dog will "die" from any position, it is time to teach "dying" from other angles. To do this you gradually reduce the amount of body posture to elicit Defense/Flight Drive. Because you will practice shooting often, your dog will quickly learn what the "Bang" command means, so that you will not need to use as much body posturing to drop your dog. Make a gradual reduction of your bending over. If your dog stops dying on the first "Bang," simply back up some and use your bending over again more carefully and don't rush eliminating it so quickly. We know your aim is not that bad, and you should always be able to shoot your dog on the first shot. Although you can always save face during a performance by claiming your aim is bad, try not to purposely teach your dog that your aim is bad. Happy shooting.

All-Star Catcher

As you know, catching something takes real hand/eye coordination. In other words it takes skill. With dogs it takes equal skill, but instead of hand/eye coordination, it takes mouth/eye coordination. With this skill you are going to teach your dog first to catch food and then balls or a favorite toy. *This trick will require some Defense Fight, enough to allow things flying through the air not to scare your dog. It will be helpful to have some Prey Drive, enough to want to catch food at least. More Prey Drive will help for catching balls and toys. Pack Drive will help to keep your dog in an attentive sitting position.*

Catching takes mouth/eye coordination.

Step 1. You will start by teaching your dog to catch a treat or a small piece of food. You can start with nuggets of your dog's dry food or small pieces of dog cookies. If these items are not interesting enough, go to cut up jerky treats or small dots of cheese. Most dogs aren't too picky.

Start with your dog facing you in a sitting position. (*See* "Move the Nose and the Body Follows" Page 70.) Step back from your dog about one to two feet. Have several pieces of food in your hand. Take one piece and show it to your dog. Then toss it UP a few inches over your dog's head as you say, "Catch." If your dog catches it, you are a very good pitcher. The skill on your part is getting the piece of food to fall, in sight, slowly towards your dog's face. By tossing the item up first, rather then directly at your dog, the food will move more slowly and your dog will have more time to focus on it. Also, it will be in the air a little longer, giving your dog a better chance to catch it.

It is better to focus your dog's attention on your hand by showing your dog the treat and then tossing it upwards on the FIRST hand motion. If you make several pretend tossing motions before throwing the food, your dog will not be able to tell exactly when the food actually leaves your hand. This will make this trick much more difficult, and that is not your intent. Help your dog to focus, then toss upwards with your catch command.

When your dog misses the treat, let him find it on the floor so you can regain his attention more quickly. If you try to grab for the missed treat, most dogs will continue to look for it, knowing they missed out on a food particle. There are few dogs who will not get to it before you anyway. True, there is valid philosophy in not allowing your dog to get a dropped treat, therefore only getting the caught ones. This philosophy intends to reward only the successes. But by rewarding the attempts—letting your dog get the dropped ones too—you will keep your dog's attention a lot longer and it will be a lot more fun for you both. Most dogs will catch on about getting the treats a lot faster when caught, rather then having to spend the time hunting for them afterwards.

If the treats are bouncing off of your dog's nose consistently, watch to see if your dog is shutting his eyes as the food comes close to his face. *This may be a product of Flight Drive.* In this case, toss the cookie so it lands in front of your dog instead of on your dog, so your dog has a chance to watch where it lands. After the eyes open to watch more closely, gradually get the cookie closer and closer until it is landing right on your dog again. By this time, your dog will realize it is okay to keep his eyes open, and you will increase the odds of your dog catching the cookie.

Another problem that can add to lots of missed catches is if the size of the cookie is too small. Try using something a little bigger like a jerky square. It is soft enough not to make your dog duck, but big enough to see well.

Step 2. Now that your dog is catching well, try to make it more challenging. First distance yourself from your dog. Say, "Catch," and back up a few extra feet making the toss three to four feet away from your dog, instead of just two feet. Try again. Keeping the distance, say, "Catch" and make the long toss. Some dogs will focus more closely if told to sit before being allowed to catch. As your tosses get farther and farther away, your pitching skill may deteriorate, so your dog will have to get up to hunt. If this gets too embarrassing, you may need to allow your dog to stand so he can make a quicker movement to continue to catch the cookie. This will make an even more impressive trick. What looks like fancy throwing may actually be just fancy catching. Your dog will understand.

Step 3. When the "Catch" command is understood because of all your training sessions using food, it is time to have your dog catch other things. It is not a good idea to switch to inedible items in the same session as one with food treats. Your dog may feel cheated and not attempt to catch after the first switch.

Start your new session with a ball or a favorite toy. Snowballs can be great fun to catch for some dogs, so be creative, but make sure it is a safe toy for your dog to catch. Begin with a distance toss. Sit

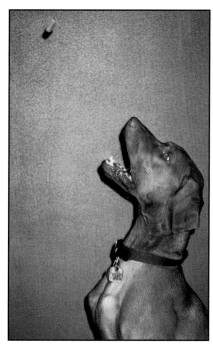

Toss a different item, such as a tennis ball, for your dog to catch.

Make the catches more challenging.

your dog, back up a few feet, show your dog the ball, say "Catch," and toss the ball. Make a really big deal about the catch and call your dog to bring the toy back to you. Have your dog give you the ball. (*See* "Take Me Out to the Ball Game: The Retrieve" Page 32.) Now sit your dog again, say "Catch," back up, and toss the ball out a few feet. *Keep trying until your dog is focusing on the ball and catching it.*

This trick is a great one for school visits and Pet Therapy sessions at nursing homes. Your dog can catch and bring back a ball without running through the halls. Other people or kids can toss the food or the balls for your dog too. Your trick training can open lots of doors for you and your dog.

Put Your Head Down

This is the sweetest of all of the tricks. If you have a little dog, it can be done while holding the dog in your arms. When you give the dog the command for "Head Down," the dog's head will drop onto your chest or shoulder and everyone in the room will get a tear and go, "Aw." If your dog is on the floor and you give the command, "Put Your Head Down, " the dog's head will go down, the eyes will look up, and everyone in the room will think you have the cutest dog in the world.

On a personal note, this is the trick my dog was doing when the man who became my husband realized that he loved me. Needless to say, *I* think this trick is a good one. It worked for me.

This is a Pack Drive trick because it takes maximum cooperation from your dog. Any dog can learn this trick, but if you have a dog with much Defense/Fight, do the Long Down exercises (Page 28) first. Actually, your dog will need to be able to do the Down and the Stay for this trick, so practice both.

Step 1.   Put your dog in the Down position on the floor. If you have a toy breed you can do this trick on a table to make it easier on your back. Praise your dog for doing the Down, even if you helped put her into position.

Step 2.   Command, "Put your head Down," and guide your dog's head to the ground with your fingers. Point to the spot between your dog's front paws as you *gently* apply a little pressure to the top of your dog's head with your other hand.

Step 3. Keep your hand on top when the dog's head is on the floor, but remember to do it gently. Praise quietly while you are doing this. It is important that your dog understands that having the head completely down is what you want. After five seconds, say "OK," and let the dog get up.

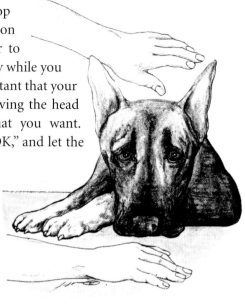

Step 4. Do steps one through three again. This time try to relax the gentle pressure holding your dog's head against the ground as you praise quietly. Relax the pressure, then replace it if the head comes up even

Don't just lay down, lay your head down too.

slightly. Praise while the head is completely down, but stop praising if the head starts to come up. After gently placing the head down again start praising.

- 🐾 Praise while the head is down, even if it is with your help.

- 🐾 Stop praising if the head starts to raise up when you relax the pressure.

- 🐾 Place the head down again, Praise.

- 🐾 Relax the pressure, and praise only while head is down.

- 🐾 Reposition the head if it comes up and start praising again.

- 🐾 So on and so on. Head down, praise. Head up, say nothing.

It is the praise at exactly the appropriate time that is teaching your dog what you are after: that is, the dog's head solidly on the floor. Practice until no pressure is required to hold your dog's head for at least five seconds. Release your dog frequently, but only if the head is completely down when you give the release word.

Step 5. Now it is time for your dog to put her head down on command *without your help*. Start with your dog in the Down position. Command "Put your head Down." Point to the ground as in step two. Do not apply your hand to the head, and wait for a few seconds. If your dog's head does not go down, then help as in step three. *Don't repeat the command, simply help.* Your dog will catch on if you have been practicing praise correctly.

Step 6. Once your dog has achieved putting her head on the ground by command, you can try doing this with your dog in your arms. Hold your dog, any way that is comfortable for you both. Command, "Put your head Down." Gently touch

Wanting to be part of the bond and the warmth.

your dog's head to your shoulder or any body part. Praise and cuddle. *(Pack Drive dogs love this exercise—so do Pack Drive people!)* Practice.

Now it is time to invite close friends over to show off the bond between you and your dog. As my husband later explained to me, "That was so special, I just wanted to be a part of that warmth."

Take a Bow

After all is said and done, and your performance is over, you must graciously accept your due applause. It is hard earned and greatly deserved. A humble performer takes a deep bow to thank the audience for such a warm, heartfelt reward. So, needless to say, you and your dog must be ready for such applause.

First of all, your dog needs to be able to Down on command. It is also helpful for your dog to know the Stay command. (*See* "Long Down" Page 28 and "Stay" Page 21.)

Step 1. First teach your dog the Stand command. Say "Stand," and with the dog on your left, put your right thumb in the collar holding the front half of your dog steady. Then put your left hand under your dog's belly and push the hind legs backwards with your left hand. Praise while your dog is standing and then release with, "OK."

Now review the Down command by telling your dog to Down. Help the dog into the Down position if necessary. Praise and then release with your "OK" release word. Review both the Stand and the Down command again.

Step 2. Stand your dog and then praise for the Stand, but don't give the release. Keep your left hand under your dog's belly as for the Stand command in step one.

Put your right hand in the collar under the dog's chin and apply a little pressure toward the ground and say, "Take a Bow." Lower the front half of your dog, and while applying the pressure under the chin, press towards the dog's elbows so that they bend rather than lock against your pressure. If necessary, use a food treat to lower the front end of your dog (*See* "Move the Nose and the Body Follows" Page 70.) Hold this position while you giggle your praise and then release and make a really big deal of how wonderfully clever your dog was, even if it was only a half bow.

Keep your left hand under your dog's belly and lower the front half of the dog with a treat (Prey) or slight pressure (Defense).

It will get better, and that is what counts. Each time it gets better, you give more praise. If it doesn't get better or improve, then don't praise as much, just say, "Let's try harder." Then try again and help your dog improve. That's the way to let your dog know what it is you are striving to do. Front half down, back end up. What a good dog. "Take A Bow."

Step 3. Stand your dog on command and praise. Keep your left hand under your dog and pat the ground in front of your dog and say, "Take a bow." Keep your left hand there to keep the rear end up. After the front end is down, try to relax your left hand under your dog's belly. Keep it nearby in case the back end slips lower. Your bows must be deep and that means the back end must be high. Remember to release and give appropriate praise and rewards.

Step 4. Stand your dog next to you. Command, "Take a Bow" and point to the ground in front of your dog. If necessary put your left hand under the dog's belly. Tell your dog to, "Stay." Take your hands off the dog and praise. If your dog gets out of the bow position, stop praising and reposition him *into* the bow. Then start praising again. It isn't necessary to reprimand at all, just position your dog into the bow again. Praise again, and after a few seconds release your dog by saying, "OK." Practice this until it isn't necessary to help your dog at all.

"May I always be the kind of person my dog thinks I am."

Step 5. Prepare for the applause to change to a standing ovation! You can bow too, if you like.

Final Note

As you practice with your dog, remember that you have a relationship of mutual trust and affection.

- 🐾 The more your dog respects you, the more the dog will love you.

- 🐾 The more time you spend with your dog, the more the dog will want to spend time with you.

🐾 The more you play with your dog, the more fun you both will have together. So make your training sessions fun.

Always end on a good note so that you will both look forward to continuing your trick training sessions again soon. Share your patience with your dog and your dog will show you how good a dog trainer you are. A magnet on my refrigerator says: "May I always be the kind of person my dog thinks I am."

Now you too can "Make it so."

Non-Sporting Dogs (All good sports!)

Glossary

A.K.C.:   The American Kennel Club is a registry of breeds recognized in the United States. The A.K.C. keeps records of bloodlines as well as titles earned by dogs in their registry. The A.K.C. is the governing body for Conformation and Performance Events in the U.S. They set the rules, approve the events, and govern the discipline at such competitions.

All-American: Mixed breed dogs are often referred to as mutts, but a much better name may be All-American because America is a melting pot of many different nationalities, just like mixed breeds.

Body Language: Body language is a powerful way to communicate with your dog. Learn how simple body motions affect your dog's Drives. Bending over your dog stimulates Defense Drive. Tilting backwards and lifting your arms stimulates Prey Drive. A neutral body posture, or kneeling next to your dog, stimulates Pack Drive. Be aware of your body. If you are not careful, you will be giving signals which are different from your spoken commands.

Breed: The canine species has different breeds which each has a Standard of perfection which may include specifics for appearance, function, and personality.

CGC (Canine Good Citizen):   The American Kennel Club has a simple test for dogs that can be given by Obedience instructors and others in your area. It tests the dog's skills for being a Canine Good Citizen. It is recognized by some as an indicator of the dog's manners. There are facilities that will only allow entrance to dogs that have a CGC certificate. The Canine Good Citizen Test evaluates your dog's ability to be under control, walk on a loose leash, follow a few simple commands, and not to be too disturbed by distractions.

Check: A check is the use of the collar and leash on your dog. A check is a short motion or quick pull that is IMMEDIATELY released so there is no more pressure on the collar. After the check, which if done correctly should *gain* your dog's attention, you need to do something to *keep* your dog's attention, like praise.

Come: The Come command should be used consistently to bring your dog directly and immediately to you. Ideally your dog should sit when he gets to you, but it is up to you whether or not you teach that step of the Come command. If the command is taught as a pleasant one, your dog should learn to come quickly and happily. You also need to work on the Come command with distractions, so that your dog will come no matter what is going on. "If you don't have a dog that comes when called, one day you won't have a dog."

Command: The command is the cue word to the dog to start an exercise or action. The command should be spoken (or signaled) clearly.

Command/Motion Sequence: It is important that you always give your command before your start a trick or exercise. Give the command before you go into motion. If you start before you command, you are expecting your dog to read your mind.

Communicate: To communicate is the ability to be understood by another. When communicating with another species (dog/human) you need to be consistent and aware of not only the spoken word, but the tone of your voice, your facial expressions, body language, and physical movements, if any.

Correct: To correct is to show your dog what you expected, but the dog did not do. For example, if your dog is jumping on you for a greeting, to correct this behavior you need to show that you want your dog sitting *on the floor* for the greeting. Correct the behavior by showing the dog the right action to do.

Crate: *See* Kennel

Defense/Fight Drive: Dog behaviors that come from the dog's natural instincts for self preservation. Some common Fight Drive behaviors are guarding territory or belongings, willingness to investigate strange new things, or not liking to be petted or groomed. Fight/Drive behaviors are activated by the need to defend yourself, your prey, or your territory.

Defense/Flight Drive: Dog behaviors that show the dog's natural insticts of self-preservation with the concern for well being. Flight/Drive is activated by the feeling of being unsure.

Dewclaw: The dewclaw is the fifth toe on the inside of the dog's leg and is generally of no use, therefore it is usually removed. In some breed Standards, it is specifically mentioned as being necessary for the breed to perform its original function. It is comparable to our thumbs.

Distemper: Canine Distemper is a highly contagious virus that attacks the gastrointestinal and respiratory tracts. It can ultimately cause neurological complications. Vaccines for this disease have all but eliminated it.

Distraction: A distraction is anything that might take your dog's attention away from the task at hand. There are different degrees of distractions. *First degree* is anything that might be going on in the area, not directed at the dog, while your dog is working or training. For example, working in the front yard with regular street activity would be first degree distractions. A *second degree* distraction is something or someone acting directly towards the dog. For example, someone kneeling nearby, talking sweetly, or asking the dog to leave to come visit. *Third degree* distractions are when food is being offered in order to tempt the dog away from the task at hand. It could also be a Frisbee flying overhead or a ball tossed near the dog. *Fourth degree* distractions are whatever is the most distracting to the dog personally. For example, to a guarding breed, someone approaching from a distance would be fourth degree. For a very high Pack Drive dog, someone touching or petting would be fourth degree.

You must train your dog to be able to work in spite of distractions. Be patient and show your dog that whatever is distracting you isn't going to change the task for you and your dog.

Dominant: Another way of looking at Defense/Fight Drive. The higher the Fight Drive the more dominant a dog would be.

Dominate: To dominate is to boss or conquer. This is not the best way to work out your relationship with your dog. This does not produce the mutual respect in a desired relationship between you and your dog.

Down: The Down should be used consistently as a command to get your dog to lay Down and remain still. When dogs are given a position command, they should not move from that position until given a release word like "OK."

Drives: Drives are different groupings of behaviors that your dog exhibits. These behaviors are instinctive and are broken into three different categories: *Prey Drive, Pack Drive,* and *Defense Drive.* Defense Drive is further subdivided into Fight/Drive and Flight/Drive. It is the concentration of these Drives that makes up your dog's personality.

Drop on Recall: This is an exercise that stops your dog from coming while en route to you. When given a "Down" command, your dog should drop to the ground without taking additional steps towards you. It is useful, for example, if something dangerous is in your dog's path. This is an exercise in Open Class Obedience when done formally.

Dumbbell: A dumbbell is an article that dogs retrieve in the Obedience show ring. It usually is a dowel with a block on each end of the dowel. The dog carries the dumbbell by the dowel. It can be made of wood or plastic.

Fecal: A fecal is a stool sample that your veterinarian would check for the presence of worms or worm eggs. Most veterinarians will want a fecal sample brought in when your dog comes for a yearly check-up.

Flea: A flea is a very prolific external parasite that lives in your dog's hair coat on the skin. A flea bite can cause your dog to itch and scratch. When your dog chews at the flea, one of the fleas might be ingested, which can cause tapeworms. Severe infections of fleas can also cause anemia because fleas suck blood when they bite your dog.

Halter (Face) Collar: A halter collar is similar to a halter for a horse and is worn on the face of the dog rather than on the neck. The idea of this type of collar is to move the nose of the dog with the thought that where the nose goes, so will the rest of the dog. The dog needs to be introduced to a halter collar in a positive manner so as not to be frightened or startled by the face collar. You should never yank on the leash while using a halter type collar.

Heartworm: A heartworm is an actual worm or parasite that lives in the dog's pulmonary artery and heart chambers. Heartworm can kill the dog if there are enough worms to block passage of the flowing blood. It is transmitted by a mosquito bite, so it is very prevalent in areas where mosquitos are.

Heel: The Heel command should be used consistently to help your dog into position at your left heel. Heel can be a moving command while walking, so that your dog walks along at your left side—no matter what direction you travel or turn into. It can also be used as a command to get your dog to move from somewhere else and *come to* your left side.

Herding Dogs: The Group of dogs that are bred to direct stock animals. Some common breeds include Belgian Sheepdog, Collie, German Shepherd Dog, Shetland Sheepdog (Sheltie), and Welsh Corgi (Pembroke and Cardigan).

Hock: The hock is the joint between the knee and the toes on the dog's hind leg. The space betwen that joint and the toes is also referred to as the hock. Appropriate angles are evaluated when a breed's conformation is discussed.

Hounds: The group of dogs that are bred to be used for hunting by use of sight or scent. Some examples include: Scenthounds; Dachshund, Basset Hound, Bloodhound, Otterhound, and Sighthounds; Greyhound, Beagle, and Whippet.

Isolate: Dog's are very social animals, especially those with much Pack Drive. Isolating your dog can be used as a powerful consequence to being too excited or out of control. But when a dog is isolated too often for too long, it can cause stress and boredom which results in destructive behavior and worse. This can be easily rectified by spending more time with your dog.

Jumps: There are three basic types of jumps. A High Jump is a solid jump usually one and a third times the dog's height at the shoulders. A Broad Jump lays on the ground in sections. It is usually twice as long as the High Jump is high. A Bar Jump is simply a stationary bar that the dog must jump rather than go under. It is usually the same height as the High Jump.

Kennel (Crate): A crate is an enclosure that your dog fits into comfortably, and used when you are unable to be with your dog. Your dog sees the crate as a den or as bedroom. *It is not a place of punishment,* but rather a napping opportunity. The size of the crate or kennel should be only large enough for your dog to lie down and turn around. *Your dog will not be exercising in it,* so keep it small enough to allow the sense of security that goes a with a den (a small enclosed shelter).

Leadership: In the natural Pack order, there is always a leader. The leader should be fair and respectful toward subordinates. With you and your dog, *you should hold the leadership position.* But remember to be fair to your dog, and the respect should flow in both directions.

Leash: A leash is a length of material used to keep your dog with you. It should be made something that you find comfortable and easy to handle. It should not be too long or awkward or folded up in your hands so that nothing is flapping in the wind (not to stimulate Prey Drive).

Leg: Leg is a term used to describe a qualifing score for any Obedience title. Each title requires three legs. People can be heard saying, "My dog has two legs towards the Novice degree (CD)."

Long Down: A Long Down is similar to a Time Out with children. It is a leadership exercise that establishes your relationship with your dog. It is not a Stay exercise, but rather a way of showing your dog that you make all of the decisions as to where, when, and for how long your dog will do something. It is a simple, fair way of showing leadership in a manner that the dog understands, and this exercise will increase and improve your relationship with your dog.

Long Sit: *See* the Long Down. The only difference is that the Long Sit is done in the sitting position for a different length of time.

Match: A match simulates a Dog Show or Obedience Trial, but is not actually the real thing. A Match is run like a Trial, but is practice to see where you are in your training and to have the experience of showing. A Fun Match can be put on by anyone and you can train in the ring if you wish. A Sanctioned Match is put on by a club associated with A.K.C., and you are not supposed to train *in* the ring, just like at a real show.

Mites: Mites are an external parasite, little insects that live on the skin. Ear mites live in the ear and can cause ear infections. Mange mites live on the skin and cause baldness and sores that can also get infected. See your veterinarian for diagnosis and treatment of mites.

Motivate: To motivate is to get your dog to do something willingly through inducement or the removal of force.

Name Proof: To Name Proof your dog during training is to teach your dog *to wait for a command following the name.* Your dog's name is not a command, simply an attention getting device used before commands.

No: This is a negative command used too often for too many things. *It should not be* used, but should be replaced by the appropriate command that redirects your dog in a positive manner. For example, if your dog is not allowed on the furniture, say "Off" instead of "No," and then direct your dog to the floor.

Non-Sporting Dogs: The group of dogs bred to be companions. Some examples include: Boston Terrier, Chow Chow, Dalmatian, Keeshond, and Lhasa Apso.

Novice [Companion Dog (CD)]: A Novice Obedience title obtainable through different agencies like A.K.C. It is the first level of Obedience. To earn this title, your dog will need to "Heel" on and off-leash, do a Recall, and perform other exercises.

Obedience: Obedience is used to name the sport of showing your dog's skill in working with you. There are three levels of Obedience: Novice, Open, and Utility.

Object of Attraction: An object of attraction is anything that dogs like enough to follow closely with their noses. Usually a small piece of food works well, but it need not be food if a toy has the same power of moving the dog's nose.

Off: Should be used consistently as a command to move your dog when your dog's feet are somewhere they should not be. This command should be used instead of "Down," *not the appropriate command if you are being consistent.* For example, when you come home and your dog jumps up on you, tell your dog "Off," and then redirect your dog into a sitting position for an appropriate greeting.

Open [Companion Dog Excellent (CDX)]:   CDX is an Open Obedience title obtainable through different agencies like A.K.C. It is the second level of Obedience. To earn the CDX title your dog will need to Heel off-leash, Drop on Recall, retrieve, jump, and do other precision exercises.

Pack Drive: Pack Drive is the set of behaviors that show the dog's willingness to be part of a pack or group. Some common behaviors would be getting along with other dogs or people, liking to be petted or groomed, and following you around the house. Pack Drive behaviors are activated by being with others *and* the hierarchy of the group.

Parvo: Parvo is a highly contagious virus that attacks the dog's gastrointestinal tract and can quickly dehydrate the animal, resulting in death. The signs of the disease are bloody diarrhea and vomiting.

Pet: A PET IS A FAMILY MEMBER. A pet should have the benefits of being part of a family as well as the rules and limitations of being in a family group. A PET SHOULD BE FOR LIFE.

Praise vs. Petting: Praise and petting are not the same thing. *Praise* is when you TELL your dog how clever he is. You should use a very happy pleasant voice that your dog responds well to. *Petting* is when you bond with your dog. Petting should take place AFTER your dog is done working, and praise should occur WHILE your dog is working.

Prey Drive: Prey Drive is the set of behaviors that show the dog's natural instincts associated with getting food when dogs lived in the wild. Some common Prey Drive behaviors would be sniffing the air or ground, stalking things in the grass, stealing food, digging, and so forth. Prey Drive behaviors are activated by sight, sound, and smell.

Prong Collar: A type of training collar that has individual links distributing the force of the correction around the dog's neck. It allows the trainer to use less force to get the attention of the dog than some other types of training collars, but should not be used unless the owner has been taught professionally how to administer corrections with such a collar.

Quick Stop: Quick Stop is a brand of styptic powder used to stop bleeding mainly when you cut your dog's nails too short. The quick in the nail is what bleeds when the nail is trimmed too closely. You should always have styptic powder handy when you cut your dog's nails.

Random: When you train using food as an inducement, you need to offer the food only as a special reward for a job well done. Do not give food for any quality of performance, dispensing it as if you were a gum ball machine. As your dog becomes better trained, you will be able to praise with your voice and then give food for a job well done, after a string of several tasks. Your dog's performance will improve if given food randomly instead of each step of the way.

Recall: The recall is a term used to describe the exercise at a dog show. The dog is left on a Sit Stay off-leash, and about 35 feet away. The dog is then called and comes to sit in front of the owner.

Registered: To have a registered dog is to have papers (a certificate) from a certified registry, like A.K.C., or through a breed club showing that the dog is purebred.

Regression: As your dog is learning something new, you can see a period of regression in skill. This usually occurs at five to six week intervals during a teaching period. Be patient, this period is a normal part of learning for a dog. Always end each training session with a positive experience, whether your dog is having a regressive experience or not.

Reinforce: To reinforce is to strengthen an association between two things. For example, to reinforce a Sit Stay, you would put your dog back into position if your dog moves from the sitting position. This reinforces the Stay command with the Sit position.

Release: The release is a word you give your dog the end of each command. If you tell your dog to sit, for example, your dog should remain in the sitting position until released. After the release you should always give your dog a reward. *See* Reward.

Rescue Dog: A rescue dog usually has had a previous home or no home, and is now being placed into what will hopefully be a permanent home. Rescue Dogs can have special needs but can be very rewarding and can make great pets.

Respect: A dog should not be completely overpowered, but rather be respected, just as you should be respected by your dog. To have a relationship of respect with your dog is to live in harmony.

Reward: A reward is compensation for a job well done A reward can be something your dog likes, like a smile or a pat for a dog with lots of Pack Drive, or a treat or ball for a dog with lots of Prey Drive.

Scent: The word scent usually defines use of the dog's nose while hunting or for locating an item. Dogs can discriminate for scent much better than we can.

Self-rewarding: Accomplishment is its own reward. For example, to a high Prey Drive dog, retrieving can be so much fun that you need not give a treat for the dog's performance. Having retrieved is self-rewarding.

Sit: The Sit command should be used consistently to get your dog to sit and sit still. A dog is given a position command should not move from that position until given a release word like "OK."

Slip Collar: A slip collar is a training collar that slips and tightens, and then slips and loosens with the use of the leash. A check on the leash tightens the collar, a slack leash loosens the slip. Also sometimes wrongly called a choke collar. The slip collar can be large enough to go over the dog's head, but then will rest too low on the dog's neck. Or the slip collar can snap around the dog's neck, helping it stay higher on the neck, therefore making it more effective.

Smile: A smile is the facial expression that you should use frequently when you are with your dog. Smiling at your dog is the body language for praise. When you find your dog looking at you, remember to smile back.

Sporting Dogs: Sporting Dogs are those in the Group bred to engage in hunting. For example, all Pointers, Retrievers, Setters, and Spaniels are Sporting Dogs.

Stand: This command should be used consistently to get your dog to stand up and stand still. When given a position command, the dog should not move from that position until given a release word, like "OK."

Stay: This command should be used consistently to get your dog to be completely still and not move from a particular position. The dog becomes a statue, and only the head or tail can move, but nothing else that is touching the ground. Stay must have a clear release word signaling that the Stay is over, for example "OK."

Stop: The Stop command should be used consistently to get the dog to quit doing something. It *should replace the word "No,"* which is over used and too negative. The *Stop command should be followed with a redirection.* For example, if your dog is chewing on the rug, say "Stop" in a firm voice and then redirect your dog's chewing with an appropriate chew toy.

Stress: The way your dog's body reacts to either mental or physical demands is called stress. The body becomes out of balance chemically. Signs of stress can be panting, pulling back the lips in a smile like grimace, or even leaving sweaty paw prints. Make sure your dog has exercise, a stable environment, and fair and humane treatment so that stress will not be a part of your dog's life.

Submissive: Submissive means low Fight Drive. Submissive behavior can also result from inhibited Flight Drive when the dog cannot run and therefore freezes in position or rolls over, exposing the belly.

Tab: A tab is a short, mini-leash that hangs from your dog's collar. It can aid you when you reach for the dog, once you have removed the regular long leash.

Tapeworm: Tapeworms are internal parasites that live in the dog's intestines. They are contracted by ingesting fleas or killing rodents. You can see the tapeworm segments in the dog's stool (fecal sample) and they look like rice or sesame seeds. They are easily treated, so see your veterinarian who will ask you to bring in a fecal specimen.

Terriers: Terriers are the Group of dogs that were bred to hunt vermin. Examples include: Airedale, Scottish, West Highland White and Cairn Terriers.

Therapy Dog: Dogs can be used in therapy for all sorts of people. The young, old, handicapped, and sick can all be cheered by the presence of a dog. A Therapy Dog will need to pass a series of tests to be certified. Check with a local training center about someone in your area who might offer this test.

Ticks: Ticks are an external parasite that attach to your dog's skin. Usually they are barely big enough to see, but if left alone, can suck enough blood to become swollen to the size of grapes. They can carry disease and should be removed safely with tweezers so as not to break off in your dog's skin.

Title: A title is an official designation given by a registry to a dog receiving appropriate amount of points or legs for a specific activity. Examples include, Champion, Companion Dog, Companion Dog Excellent, etc.

Tone of Voice: Your voice alone can change your dog's Drive; a soothing quiet voice for Pack Drive, a quick, high pitched voice for Prey Drive, and a loud, low, harsh voice for Defense Drive. Make sure you use the tone of voice that you intend when communicating with your dog.

Toy Breeds: Toy breeds are the Group bred for their small size. Examples include: Chihuahua, Maltese, Pomeranian, Toy Poodle, Yorkshire Terrier, and Shih Tzu.

Training Collar: A training collar is a collar that is used with a leash to connect you with your dog and to getyour dog's attention when used correctly. It can be anything from a regular buckle collar or a slip collar to a halter face collar made of various materials.

Treat: A treat is a small piece of food to give your dog as a reward. It should be big enough to be enticing, but so small that it is instantly gone.

Trial: A Trial is a show held an official licensing organization for points or legs towards Obedience titles.

Utility (UD): UD is an Obedience title and obtainable through various licensing agencies like A.K.C. It is the highest class level of Obedience. To qualify for the Utility title, your dog will need to do Hand Signals, Scent Discrimination, jumping, and other precision exercises.

Wait: The wait command should be used consistently to tell your dog *not to* progress or move forward. It is not a Stay, during which the dog can't move, but rather just a command not to go ahead just yet, for example, through a doorway.

Withers: Withers are the highest part of the shoulder blades, right behind the neck. This is where a dog's height is usually measured

Working Dogs: Working dogs are the Group bred to do a specific job. Examples include: Akita, Boxer, Doberman Pinscher, St. Bernard.